What Leaders are Saying about The Total Control QRP

"For years, the lack of control I had over my OWN MONEY in my 401k was a serious source of frustration for me. I've always viewed the stock market as a form of gambling, so I didn't want to send my money to Wall Street—and I don't like bonds or treasury notes, because of out of control government spending. So that left only 1 choice inside my 401k… Cash. As a result, years went by with my entire 401k being 100% stuck in cash, and as the government continued to print more and more cash, my retirement account got less and less valuable, and I got more and more frustrated.

All that changed in 2012. I met Damion Lupo and learned about the QRP. After I had my attorney thoroughly scrutinize the plan and give me a double thumbs up approval I got my own QRP set up and took CHECK-BOOK CONTROL of my own money. Now my retirement money is 100% MINE to invest the way I want.

If you're anything like me you absolutely owe it to yourself to get a QRP!"

Jon Butcher
Chairman, Precious Moments Inc.

"Damion's team have been exceptional in putting together and helping me get my QRP set up! I have comfort in knowing that I have control over my money and best of all I don't have to deal with cumbersome paperwork every single year!"

Dr. Angelica Farrell
Chiropractor / Business Owner, Salud Chiropractic

The Total Control Financial
Guide to the Q.R.P.

How to get Checkbook Control of your ROLLOVER 401(k) Money NOW!

DAMION S. LUPO
&
JOHN P. D'ARCO, ESQ.

The Total Control Financial Guide to the Q.R.P. - How to get total CHECKBOOK CONTROL of Your ROLLOVER 401K Money Now!

Inquiries should be addressed to:

Total Control Financial LLC
12407 MoPac Expwy. N.
#250-405
Austin, Texas 78758

www.TheQRPBook.com

First Edition

First Printing 4-15-16

Cover design by: Cornelia Murariu

ISBN print   978-1-945057-00-7
ISBN electronic   978-1-945057-01-4

1. Retirement Plans 2. Financial

Dear Investor,

Congratulations on taking this powerful step towards TOTAL CONTROL of your FINANCIAL FUTURE! This is one of the most important Self Responsible choices you will ever make!

One of the greatest tragedies for most Americans is the restrictive nature of the tax code forcing most to needlessly pay too much in taxes and shortchanging their retirement accounts when they could be doing the opposite, using the code to get rich.

Doing what Wall Street suggests you do often leads to a disastrous "retirement" without enough resources to live on and a reliance on government programs and charity.

That is not your path. That is not your future.

The solution to this problem for the Self-Responsible person is the Total Control QRP. This is a tool that fully utilizes the tax code to your advantage and cuts the bankers and brokers out. It gives **you** power and control to build and control your retirement wealth on your terms.

This book outlines how you can take advantage of legal strategies to pay less taxes and compound your wealth into a much bigger retirement nest egg than you could without using the QRP.

The biggest advantage to having your own QRP is the **checkbook control** you get. Your money is truly in your control and you get to choose how, when and where you invest it with almost unlimited options. **YOU ARE NO LONGER STUCK with the WALL STREET JUNK!**

You simply do not have that choice when your retirement money is being handled by the Wall Street Brokerages and Banks. Why?

They don't want you to control it! Once you get control they lose control and **they forever lose the ability to charge fees!**

Bad for the bank, but good for you!

Whether you want to invest in physical gold and silver, real estate or one of the other powerful investment options available with your Total Control QRP - if you want to be in the driver seat and control your own retirement money - read this book and set up your QRP today.

Having a Total Control QRP is one of the smartest things you will ever do for the safety and security of your future!

I commend you for taking full responsibility and for taking action today!!

Very Truly Yours,

Damion S. Lupo

Please Read

This book is designed to provide general information pertaining to the subjects discussed including retirement accounts. Laws and general practices vary from state to state and change constantly. With each situation different, specific advice for specific situations should be obtained by the reader's own advisors pertaining to the reader's situation.

The author has taken reasonable precautions in preparing this book and believes the facts are accurate as of the date it was written. Many of the thoughts, ideas and opinions are subjective and relevant to the current environment. They could change based any number of evolving environments, laws and geo political shifts. Neither the author nor publisher assumes any responsibility for any errors or omissions. The author and publisher specifically disclaim any liability resulting from the use or application of the information contained in this book, and the information is not intended to serve as legal advice related to individual situations.

The author highly recommends you consult with your advisors, including your attorney and accountant about any plans you may have or are considering and that you get their professional opinion and advice before taking any action.

Table of Contents

INTRODUCTION. 13

SECTION 1: THE DETAILS

QUALIFIED RETIREMENT PLANS 19
    Where did the QRP come from? 19
    Learning Objectives. 19
    Introduction. 19
    What is a QRP? 21

TYPES OF BENEFIT PLANS. 23
    Non-Qualified Plans 23
    Why Haven't I Heard of the QRP? 23
    General Features of All Qualified Retirement Plans 24

RETIREMENT PLAN TYPES 25
    401(k) Plan. 25

THE QUALIFIED PLANS FOR
SELF-EMPLOYED INDIVIDUALS 27
    One Person 401(k) Plan 27
    Roth 401(k) 27

QRP PLAN FEATURES. 35
    Borrowing from the Plan. 35
    Loan Restrictions and Limitations 35
    Interest Deduction Limitations. 36
    Loans From 401(k) Plans 37
    Withdrawals. 37
    In-Service Distributions 38
    Early Distributions and Exceptions 39
    Divorce Payments 41

Asset Protection 42
Other Reporting Requirements for All Taxpayers 43

PERMITTED INVESTMENTS **45**
Here is a List of Some Examples of What
    You Can Use Your QRP to Invest In 45
Life Insurance 46
Who May Be Involved in Your Investment Decision 46
Real Estate 47
Precious Metals—GOLD, SILVER & PLATINUM 49

DISALLOWED INVESTMENTS &
PROHIBITED TRANSACTIONS **53**
Disallowed Investments 53
Prohibited Transactions 53
Prohibited Transactions Between Disqualified Persons: . . . 54
Avoiding Prohibited Transactions 55
Exemptions 55

ESTABLISHING A QRP **57**

QRP ADMINISTRATION **59**
Information Returns 59

SAVERS CREDIT **61**

TAX ALERTS **63**

THE 8TH WONDER OF THE WORLD **65**

SECTION 2

QRP VS. ET.AL **71**

SECTION 3

THE ROLLOVER QRP 77
   Disallowed Investments and Disqualified Persons 78
   How to Get a QRP Even if You're Broke 79

SECTION 4

THE REAL ESTATE INVESTOR 83

SECTION 5

THE QRP DICTIONARY 93
ARTICLES 117

SECTION 6

FAQ'S 123

Introduction

This book is laid out for you to blast through it and get high level concepts about the QRP in about 30-60 minutes. You'll also find a lot of additional information and resources with more detail and nuances and references that you can use to dig deeper into the material. The end of the book is full of frequently asked questions commonly asked about the QRP. You can also visit *www.TheQRP. org* for additional information and to ask specific questions with the interactive information site.

The next page is a flow chart if you want to get right to the most relevant QRP for you. If you want to know what type of QRP to set up and how to set it up, go straight to the farmyard and identify your animal. If you get to the chapter that fits your situation and you have questions, jump to the FAQ's and definitions. Those will clear up most questions. Still have questions? Send us an email or call us anytime!

The Dirty path is a longer, but more thorough path that will give you a lot more of the nitty gritty details about a QRP. You'll likely get more information than you know what to do with. You will have enough to run your own retirement plan and enough to have a high level conversation with your attorney, accountant or other third party administrator. Feel free to jump right to the section most appropriate to what you need. This book is by no means meant to be read from front to back like a novel.

The dirty details starts with section one, which will give you a brief look at all aspects of the retirement plans available and compare the different ideas and options. You will know more than many financial advisors when you're done!! Then you can go to the farmyard and see which animal fits your situation. If you have any questions on your journey for knowledge, you will have even more information in the FAQ's and Definitions sections.

Thank you for your time and attention and happy investing!

Respectfully,

Damion S. Lupo

John P. D'Arco,
Tax Attorney & CPA

Section 1

The Details

"Everything popular is wrong."

—Oscar Wilde

Wall Street Propaganda: The Spring 2012 issue of Charles Schwab's investing newsletter includes an article on 401(k)s and states:

> "IRAs offer more flexibility than 401(k)s when it comes to investment options. A typical 401(k) plan provides no more than two dozen funds choices, compared to thousands of fund possibilities in an IRA. You may, however, be subject to annual fees or minimum balance requirements. When you stay with your 401(k), you are limited to what your former employer offers."

The **key** piece of information the author leaves out is that when you have a Total Control QRP, which is effectively a self directed 401(k) you have way more flexibility, control and protection that any form or version of an IRA. But they wouldn't want you to know that. We do.

> "The age old idea of putting money into the stock markets and getting an 8-10% fixed reliable return without being savvy, i.e. "passive dumb income" is a dead idea. Those days are over."

—Bill Gross, PIMCO

Qualified Retirement Plans for Small Businesses

WHERE DID THE QRP COME FROM?

The purpose of this book is to provide you with a knowledge and understanding of the various retirement plan options available. From a previous employee this manual will provide you with the opportunity to learn about the many tax advantages of retirement plans and features of qualified plans that can reduce both the cost and complexity of implementing and maintaining one.

LEARNING OBJECTIVES

After reading this book you will be able to:

❑ Compare the advantages and disadvantages of qualified and non-qualified retirement plans.
❑ Analyze the tax and non tax benefits of a qualified retirement plan.
❑ List the basic steps in establishing a qualified retirement plan.
❑ Contrast features of the various types of plans.
❑ Describe the basic requirements of maintaining a qualified retirement plan.

INTRODUCTION

Today, the American dream is to have the ability to set aside funds to plan for retirement and unforeseen financial emergencies. However, in today's ever changing economy, finding the extra money to save for the future may seem impossible for many workers. This is especially difficult for those employed in small businesses.

Today, more than ever, Americans realize the importance of saving for the future. Most experts estimate that the average American will need between $1.2 million to $1.5 million in a retirement plan to provide for a reasonable lifestyle after retirement. They also estimate that 8 months of expenses should be put aside for unexpected financial emergencies or about $30,000 to $50,000 for the average worker.

In order to provide American workers the opportunity to save and plan for retirement, the U.S. Internal Revenue Code provides a variety of tax-advantage retirement plans through which employees may save funds for retirement. In addition, employers can offer retirement plans for employees' that, if they meet certain qualifications under the Tax Code, create tax advantages for both parties.

However, with any qualified retirement savings plan for which the government affords tax breaks, there are requirements, under the current tax code and the *Employee Retirement Income Security Act of 1974 (ERISA)*, for maintaining the plans. For example, plans must be updated to reflect changes in the law and information about the plan must be reported annually to employees as well as the IRS. If a plan falls out of compliance or is inappropriately used for the advantage of the wrong parties, it must be corrected to avoid penalties or the loss of its qualification for special tax treatment.

This section describes the various types of plans which may be appropriate, taking into account the employer's particular resources and objectives. Some qualified plans, called **defined benefit plans,** are structured so that the employee is guaranteed to receive a specific amount of benefits upon retirement, and require employers to make contributions.

WHAT IS A QRP?

The QRP is a Qualified Retirement Plan. The Internal Revenue Code (Section 401) defines it as a retirement savings trust. The difference between a Qualified and Non-Qualified Plan:

A qualified plan is a type of retirement savings plan set up by a business that conforms to the requirements of Section 401 of the U.S. Tax code. Since a qualified retirement plan conforms to Section 401 requirements, the plan qualifies for special tax rules that provide small business owners with substantial tax saving opportunities. Some of the most common types of qualified plans are Profit Sharing Plans, 401(k) plans, and Defined Benefit Plans. One of the biggest advantages is that contributions made by the employer to the plan on behalf of the employee are tax deductible. Contributions are made using pre-tax dollars which allows you to postpone paying income taxes on money contributed giving it time to compound and grow over time. Under ERISA (Employee Retirement Income Security ACT) of 1974, qualified plan investments are protected from creditors, bankruptcy, and the IRS.

The Rollover QRP and the Real Estate QRP are the Ferraris of 401(k)'s because of the way it written. They are written to give you every option allowable by law and approved by the IRS. You can truly do anything you want within the framework of what's allowed by law.

Types of Benefit Plans

NON-QUALIFIED PLANS

Plans that do not follow the guidelines and rules Congress has passed into law and thus cannot take advantage of most of the benefits a qualified plan can. (i.e. deferred compensation plans)

WHY HAVEN'T I HEARD OF THE QRP?

The investment industry has been dominated by 3rd party custodians who have large transaction fees and have limited the investment choices. As trustee of these types of retirement plans, they make money charging transactional and management fees to perform trustee duties. With a QRP, you are the trustee and eliminate investment decisions that most likely are not the best for your business and you will also eliminate transactional and management fees that add up over time.

It has also been a misconception over the last 30 years that stocks are the best investments, when in fact a portfolio that is diverse with many types of investments will yield the best return. Your QRP could be designed to allow you as trustee giving you checkbook control and the authority to invest in alternative investments such as gold and silver, tax liens, business start ups, real estate, LLC's, joint ventures, etc.

GENERAL FEATURES OF ALL QUALIFIED RETIREMENT PLANS

Asset Protection

As mentioned previously, assets held in a qualified retirement plan are required to contain "anti alienation" provisions under ERISA. Therefore, pursuant to bankruptcy laws, employer and employee assets in qualified retirement plans are generally protected from creditors including the IRS. I recommend you discuss this with your tax advisor as every situation is different.

Retirement Plan Types

There are two main categories of plans; defined benefit plans and defined contribution plans.

401(k) PLAN

A 401(k) plan is a qualified retirement plan that is funded primarily through employee contributions via salary reductions. It was legislatively created in 1978, and by 1981, half of all large corporations had adopted them. Today, use of 401(k)'s is not exclusive to large corporations; even a sole proprietor with no employees can use a 401(k). Through a 401(k) plan, companies have the option to make matching contributions, which vest for participants in the same manner as contributions to other defined contribution plans explained earlier.

Perhaps the most popular type of defined contribution plan today is the 401(k) plan. The 401(k) plan allows employee contributions to be made through salary reduction arrangements that let them fund their retirement plan with pretax dollars. These employee contributions are called **elective deferrals**. Employers often match a percentage of employee elective deferrals as a way to encourage participation, something desirable so that owners, executives, and other highly paid employees can benefit. In addition to pretax contributions, a 401(k) plan may offer a Roth contribution option.

Qualified Plans for Individuals

THE ONE PERSON 401(k) PLAN

Even if you work alone, with no employees, you can still have a 401(k) plan. In 2001 Congress passed EGTRRA which made this possible. This type of plan may enable you to maximize contributions because you can make both employee salary reduction contributions (elective deferrals) and employer contributions.

ROTH 401(k)

A Roth 401(k) plan is a separate account through which a participant will make designated after-tax contributions. A Roth 401(k) plan combines the unique features of the Roth IRA and a traditional 401(k) plan. The main difference between a Roth 401(k) and a traditional 401(k) is that the Roth 401(k) is funded with after-tax dollars and the traditional 401(k) plan is funded with pre-tax dollars. While the Roth 401(k) doesn't get the same upfront tax-deduction as the traditional 401(k), the account grows tax-free. Withdrawals taken during retirement are NOT subject to income tax as long as you've had the account for five or more years and are 59 ½ or older.

Key advantages of a Roth 401(k):

- ❑ Annual contribution limits are much higher than in a Roth IRA.
- ❑ No modified gross income limitations that restrict some individuals from contributing to a Roth IRA.
- ❑ Participants can keep BOTH pre-tax and after-tax (Roth) savings in a single plan.

A participant may convert their 401(k) to a Roth 401(k) commonly called an in-plan rollover. Some guidelines are:

- ❏ Only eligible rollover distributions may convert; typically rollovers or age 59 ½.
- ❏ The plan must allow for in-plan Roth conversions and Roth contributions.
- ❏ Tax paid on amounts converted to Roth (10% tax prior to 59 ½ not applicable)

ROTH 401(k) Eligibility

Anyone, regardless of income level, can have a ROTH, as long as the company plan offers it. The QRP comes standard with a ROTH option. Plan participants can choose to have pre-tax or post-tax (Roth) contributions for their elective deferrals.

Separate accounting is required for the Roth 401(k).

ROTH 401(k) Contributions

A Roth 401(k) plan may permit a participant to contribute some or all of their elective deferrals as after-tax contributions. In order to permit after-tax contributions, the plan document must include a choice of both pre-tax and after-tax(Roth) elective deferrals, separate accounts for designated Roth contributions, and must state that only Roth elective deferrals can be contributed to the designated Roth account.

A plan participant has the option to make elective deferrals to the designated Roth account, pre-tax account, or both in whatever increments and proportions they choose as permitted under the plan terms. Total contributions for the Roth account and pre-tax elective deferral cannot exceed the plan annual contribution limit.

One of the biggest advantages of a Roth 401(k) is that there are no income restrictions. This is very appealing for high-income individuals who haven't been able to contribute to a Roth IRA because of income restrictions. Like a traditional 401(k) plan, Roth 401(k) plans are subject to the same contribution limits, which is $18,000 in 2013 and $24,000 for those 50 or older. Roth IRA contributions limits are much less than the Roth 401(k) ($5,500 per year and $6,500 if you are 50 or older). Due to the fact that Roth 401(k) plans are not constrained to the same income restrictions as a Roth IRA, participants can invest thousands of dollars more in tax-free retirement income that the Roth IRA.

Roth 401(k) contributions are treated the same as pre-tax elective deferrals in the following ways:

- ❑ Annual contribution limits
- ❑ Mandatory minimum distributions
- ❑ Distribution restrictions
- ❑ Nondiscrimination testing
- ❑ Plan deduction limits (calculation)

Roth 401(k) contributions are irrevocable, meaning that once contributions are invested into a Roth 401(k) account, it cannot be moved to a regular 401(k) account.

A participant cannot make contributions to a Roth 401(k) for a spouse who has no earned income. A traditional or Roth IRA will allow for a participant to make contributions for your spouse based on their earned income.

Upon termination, a participant may roll the Roth 401(k) into a Roth IRA.

ROTH 401(K) Distributions

A qualified distribution is not included in your gross income and is generally made after the 5 taxable year period of participation. A distribution is considered a qualified distribution when one of the following criteria are met:

- ❑ The distribution occurs on or after the date you attain age 59 ½.
- ❑ The distribution occurs after your death.
- ❑ The distribution is attributable to you being disabled.
- ❑ You have held the plan for more than 5 years.

It is important to note that distributions that are out of the participant's control, such as plan termination or job termination, are NOT considered qualified distributions (unless you meet one of the qualified distribution criteria listed above). However, in situations like this, you do have the option to do a direct rollover into another designated Roth account.

A non-qualified, in other words, a premature distribution, is subject to the following:

A 10% tax penalty may apply on early withdrawals to the part of the distribution that is included in gross income.

The distribution will be handled as pro-rata from earnings and contributions (basis).

The following distributions are not considered qualified and will include any earnings paid out in gross income:

- ❑ Corrective distribution of elective deferrals in excess of the lesser of $50,500 (2013) or 100% earnings.
- ❑ Deemed distributions from a default on repayment of a loan from the plan.

- ❑ Corrective distributions of excess deferrals. ($17,500 and $23,300 in 2013 if over age 50).
- ❑ Corrective distributions of excess contributions.

The 5 taxable year period begins on the first day of your taxable year for which you made the first contribution to the Roth 401(k) plan. However, if you rollover from a designated Roth account under another plan, the 5 year period begins on the first day of the taxable year that you made designated Roth contributions to the other plan (if this date is earlier than the other).

If you receive a distribution before the 5 taxable year period, it will be considered a non qualified distribution and the earnings must be included in your gross income. Early withdrawals from a Roth 401(k) are subject to the same rules and requirements as a traditional 401(k) that we will discuss in the Plan Features section. For the withdrawal to avoid taxation, it must be a qualified distribution and occur at least 5 years from the first Roth 401(k) contribution or predecessor Roth 401(k) contribution. Roth 401(k) contributions will show as deferrals on a W2 and the distributions are reported on Form 1099-R.

Many assume that since contributions to a Roth 401(k) are from after-tax income, that you can make tax-free withdrawals at any time. This is not allowed. The same restrictions apply to Roth 401(k) withdrawals that apply to pre-tax elective contributions. If your plan permits a hardship withdrawal, the distribution earnings portion will be included in your gross income unless you have had the account for 5 years, are age 59 ½, or disabled.

A Roth 401(k) has minimum distribution requirements a participant must begin to receive annually once he/she is the later age of 70 ½ or retires.

ROTH 401(K) Loans

If the plan permits, YES you can take a loan from a Roth 401(k). There are guidelines that must be followed in determining the loan amount. A loan from your plan must be combined with all other outstanding loans from the plan and any other plans maintained by the employer.

ROTH 401(k) In-Plan Rollover

If the plan allows, a participant may transfer eligible rollover distributions to a designated Roth account from another account in the same plan. It is important to note that in order for the plan to accept in-plan rollovers, it MUST be set up to accept elective deferrals from participants. You cannot set up a plan to solely accept in-plan rollovers.

Eligible In-Plan Rollovers

The terms of the plan and other eligible distribution rules will determine the eligible rollover amount. Not all pre-tax balances can be rolled into a Roth 401(k) plan. An eligible rollover distribution is a distribution that is NOT the following:

- ❑ Hardship distribution
- ❑ Required minimum distribution
- ❑ A loan treated as a distribution
- ❑ A distribution that is one of a series of substantially equal payments made for 10 years or a minimum of once a year over a lifetime.
- ❑ A corrective distribution of excess contributions or deferrals
- ❑ Dividends on employer securities
- ❑ The cost of life insurance

In-Plan Rollover Tax Consequences

An in-plan rollover is not subject to the additional 10% early withdrawal tax. If the rollover is withdrawn from the designated Roth account within five years it could be subject to this tax.

The taxable amount of the rollover distribution must be included in the participant's gross income. This is calculated by taking the value of the distribution less the participant's basis. Typically, the entire rollover amount including earnings from a pre-tax account will be taxable. Generally, a plan participant must include any previously untaxed amounts in gross income during the year the rollover occurred.

Once the rollover is complete to a designated Roth 401(k) plan, it cannot be reversed. The rollover amount cannot be re-characterized or returned to the account it came from.

ROTH 401(k) VS Traditional 401(k)

When deciding between a Roth 401(k) and a traditional 401(k), many ask themselves, "Do I take a pay cut and invest in a ROTH 401(k) since contributions are made with after-tax dollars? OR Invest in a traditional 401(k) and have the tax dollars taken out when I receive distributions at retirement?" If you think you will be in a higher tax bracket at the time of retirement, then it would make sense to invest in a Roth IRA. If you are near retirement age and figure your tax bracket will be lower in retirement, you will benefit from making traditional 401(k) contributions. Roth 401(k) plans are desirable to those in high tax brackets who want to pay the taxes now in exchange for the certainty they won't have to pay taxes in the future no matter what tax bracket they are in upon retirement age.

If you still can't decide which plan to invest in, you can invest in both a Roth 401(k) and a traditional 401(k) plan in the same year in any proportion you decide.

ROTH

A huge difference between an IRA and the QRP is for the high earner. Once you reach a certain income level you can not contribute to a Roth IRA or convert a standard IRA to a Roth IRA. You do not have this limitation with the QRP. You're welcome to contribute up to $18,000 per year into a Roth sub-account of your QRP, or $24,000 if you're over age 50. You can have both a Roth and regular tax deferral component within the QRP.

QRP Plan Features

BORROWING FROM THE PLAN

Within limits, owners may be able to borrow from the plan without adverse tax consequences. The plan must permit loans, limiting them to the lesser of:

- ❑ $50,000 or
- ❑ The greater of one-half your accrued benefit or $10,000

Loans that do not meet the limits above are treated as taxable distributions from the plan. If this occurs, you will receive Form 1099-R.

The loan must be amortized over a period of no more than five years (except for loans that are used to buy personal residences) and charge a reasonable rate of interest. Quarterly payments should be made in substantially equal amounts. You can however make more frequent payments such as monthly payments. It is important to remember that loan repayments are NOT plan contributions.

As an owner, you cannot deduct interest on the loan but the plan pays no tax on the interest income either. The plan must also allow rank-and-file employees the opportunity to borrow from the plan on the same basis as owners and top executives.

LOAN RESTRICTIONS AND LIMITATIONS

- ❑ **Spousal consent** is generally required for loan approval.
- ❑ **If the vested accrued benefit = $20,000 or less:**

  - You are not taxed on the loan, when added to all other outstanding loans amounts to $10,000 or less.

- The maximum loan may not exceed 50% of your vested account balance. The Labor Department only allows up to 50% of the vested balance to be 119used as loan security. If additional collateral is provided, loans in excess of the 50% cap are allowed.

❏ **If the vested accrued benefit is greater than $20,000:**

- You will not be taxed on a loan that does not exceed the lesser of $50,000 or 50% of the vested benefit, as long as you did not borrow from any employer plan within a one-year period ending on the day before the date of the new loan.
- If you borrowed within the one-year period, the $50,000 limit will be further reduced. The maximum loan limit is calculated by the difference between highest outstanding balance of all loans during the one-year period ending the day before the new loan and the outstanding balance of the participant's loans from the plan on the date of the new loan.

INTEREST DEDUCTION LIMITATIONS

If you are not a key employee and want to borrow from your account to purchase a first or second residence, you can generally obtain a full interest deduction by using the residence as collateral for the loan. Your account balance may not be used to secure the loan. Interest deductions for plan loans are not allowed for key employees

If you are not a key employee and use the plan for investment purposes, and the loan is not secured by your elective deferrals or allocable income to a 401(k) plan, the loan account interest is deductible up to investment income. Unless your residence is the security for the loan, interest on loans used for personal purposes is not deductible.

LOANS FROM 401(k) PLANS

The rules governing loans from 401(k) plans are the same as those discussed above. It should be noted that all participants, not just owners, are prohibited from deducting interest on plan loans. However, the interest is really being paid to the participant's own account, so the loss of a deduction is not as important.

For more information see: *IRS Publication 575*

WITHDRAWALS

Amounts attributable to elective deferrals and qualified non-elective deferrals may not be distributed earlier than:

- ❑ Separation from service (termination, discharge, death or disability).
- ❑ Termination of the plan without the establishment or maintenance of another defined contribution plan (except an ESOP).
- ❑ The attainment of age 59 ½ (profit sharing and stock bonus plans only).
- ❑ Hardship of the employee.

HARDSHIP WITHDRAWALS

While hardship withdrawals are permitted, there are some rules and employer must follow if permitting the withdrawals. First, the plan documents must permit hardship withdrawals. Second, the amount of hardship withdrawal is limited to the employee's deferral amounts, generally without earnings. Third, they may be made under the following conditions:

- ❑ It is not permissible to withdraw employer contributions in a hardship withdrawal,

❑ A hardship distribution is limited to the amount that will satisfy an immediate and financial need of the employee. IRS regulation states that an immediate and heavy financial need is:

- Expenses for medical care (as defined in IRC §213(d) previously incurred by the employee or his or her spouse or dependents or necessary for these persons to obtain medical care,
- Costs directly related to the purchase of a principal residence for the employee (excluding mortgage payments),
- Payment of tuition, related educational fees, and room and board expenses for the next 12 months of post-secondary education for the employee or the employee's spouse, children or dependents, or
- Payment necessary to prevent the eviction of the employee from his or her principal residence or foreclosure on the mortgage of the employee's principal residence.

IN-SERVICE DISTRIBUTIONS

The law will allow you to take distributions in very limited circumstances from your profit sharing plan while your business is still in operation. The limited circumstances under which you can take in-service distributions are the following:

❑ A distribution to a participant after he or she has participated in the plan for a fixed number of years, usually at least two.
❑ A distribution after the participant attains a stated age. (The age is generally set by the plan.)
❑ A distribution to a participant upon the occurrence of some event, such as layoff, illness, disability, retirement, death or termination of employment.

- ❑ In-Service Distributions are generally not a taxable event if the distribution is done to rollover your funds into another qualified plan.

EARLY DISTRIBUTIONS AND EXCEPTIONS

Any distribution (other than a rollover) you take from your profit sharing plan before you reach age 59 ½ is considered an early distribution, which means you must pay a 10% penalty in addition to income tax unless an exception applies. The exceptions will eliminate the penalty, but not the income tax. Exceptions include:

- ❑ **Death:** Distribution from your profit sharing plan after you die is not subject to the early distribution penalty, no matter how old you are when you die or how old your beneficiaries are when they withdraw the money.
- ❑ **Disability:** If you become disabled, you can take money from your profit sharing plan without penalty. But first you must satisfy the IRS's definition of disabled, which can be difficult. It reads: "You must be unable to engage in any substantial gainful activity by reason of any medical determinable physical or mental impairment which can be expected to result in death or to be of long-continued and indefinite duration." The IRS's own regulations state that the gainful activity refers specially to the type of work you were doing before becoming disabled. Thus it would seem that you need not be unfit for all work; just the work you customarily do.
- ❑ **Periodic Payments:** You can begin taking distributions from your self-employed plan regardless of your age as long as you take them in equal annual installments over your life expectancy.
- ❑ **Leaving Your Business after Age 55:** If you are at least 55 years old when you leave or terminate your business, any distributions you receive from your profit sharing plan will not be subject to an early distribution penalty.

- ❑ **QDRO Payments:** If you are paying child support or alimony from your retirement plan, or if you intend to distribute some or the entire plan to your former spouse as part of a property settlement, none of those payments are subject to the early distribution penalty as long as there is a QDRO in place that orders the payments. (See Section 4, above, for more information about QDROs).

- ❑ **Refunds:** If you contributed more to your profit sharing plan than you were permitted to deduct during the year, generally you can remove the excess without penalty if you do so before you file your tax return.

- ❑ **Mandatory Distributions:** If you own your own business, you must start taking money out of your profit sharing plan beginning in the year you turn 70 ½ even if you are still working. If you are still working when your reach 70 ½, you may continue to make contributions to a profit sharing plan and deduct those contributions. It could very well make sense for you to do so even though you are also required to take some money out each year.

- ❑ **Medical Expenses:** Although you can take money out of your profit sharing plan prior to age 59 ½ to pay for medical expenses, you won't escape the penalty entirely. The exemption applies only to the portion of your medical expenses that would be deductible on Schedule A of your tax return if you were to itemize deductions (whether or not you actually do itemize deductions). The remainder is subject to penalty.

EXAMPLE: Your adjusted gross income of $50,000. You had medical bills of $6,000 during the year, which you paid with funds you withdrew from your profit sharing plan. (The $6,000 distribution is included in the $50,000 of income.) For income tax purposes, you are permitted to deduct medical expenses that exceed 7.5% of your adjusted gross income. Thus: Adjusted gross income (AGI, including the profit sharing plan distribution =

$50,000; 7.5% of AGI (.075 x $50,000) = $3,750 nondeductible expense; Excess ($6,000 - $3,750) = $2,250 deductible expenses.

Although you took $6,000 from your profit sharing plan to pay medical expenses, only $2,250 will escape the early distribution penalty. The remaining $3,750 will be subject to the penalty (unless you qualify for another exception), and the entire $6000 is subject to regular income tax.

DIVORCE PAYMENTS

Congress has passed legislation to protect your self-employed plan assets. The key protection provision is known as the "anti-alienation" rule, which attempts to ensure that you (the plan participant) cannot voluntarily or involuntarily transfer your interest in plan assets to another person or entity. However, divorce is a unique situation. What if you must use your retirement plan as part of a property settlement? Can you transfer some or all of your interest in the plan assets in this situation? And if you can, who should be responsible for the taxes and penalties (if any) on the part you transfer?

Congress addressed these concerns by giving divorcing couples a vehicle for protecting plan assets and minimizing tax and penalties. It's called a Qualified Domestic Relations Order or QDRO. The QDRO rules spell out the circumstances under which your qualified plan benefits can go to someone else such as your soon-to-be former spouse. These rules also provide liability protection to the trustee who distributes the assets under the terms of the QDRO. A QDRO is a judgment, decree, or order (including a court approved property settlement agreement) that satisfies all of the following requirements:

❑ It contains certain language, specifically:

- The alternate payee must be referred to as "the alternate payee" in the QDRO
- The QDRO must identify the plan, as well as the amount of each payment and the number of payments to be made.
- The QDRO must contain the name and address of both you and the alternate payee.

❑ It relates to child support, alimony or martial property rights of your spouse, dependent child or some other dependent.

❑ It gives an alternate payee, such as a spouse, former spouse, dependent child or other dependent, the right to receive all or a portion of your plan benefits.

❑ It does not alter the form or the amount of the benefit originally intended for you, even though the benefit might now go to an alternate payee. For example, the QDRO cannot require the plan to pay a larger annuity to the alternate payee than it would have paid to you.

If you have a QDRO in place, the law will allow the trustee of the plan to distribute to the alternate payee his or her share of you plan assets without disqualifying the plan-as long as the plan also permits distribution. And generally, he or she will be responsible for any income taxes on the distributions he or she receives.

ASSET PROTECTION

As mentioned previously, assets held in a qualified retirement plan are required to contain "anti alienation" provisions under ERISA. Therefore, pursuant to bankruptcy laws, employer and employee assets in qualified retirement plans are generally protected from creditors including the IRS. I recommend you discuss this with your tax advisor as every situation is different.

OTHER REPORTING REQUIREMENTS FOR ALL TAXPAYERS

Qualified plans have annual reporting requirements which state you must file certain information returns each year to report on the amount of plan assets, contributions, number of employees, and such (unless you are exempt from reporting). Information returns in the Form 5500 series are not filed with the IRS. Instead, these returns are filed with the Department of Labor's Pension and Welfare Benefits Administration (PWBA). With the exception of one person plans, all plans must file Form 5500, Annual Return/Report of Employee Benefit Plan each year. The return is due by the last day of the seventh month following the close of the plan year (July 31 for a calendar year plan).

Single participant plans are automatically exempt from annual reporting if the plan assets at the end of the year are $250,000 or less.

Form 1099R and Form 945 are also required for participant distributions.

Permitted Investments

HERE IS A LIST OF SOME EXAMPLES OF WHAT YOU CAN USE YOUR QRP TO INVEST IN:

- ❑ Gold Bullion coins and bars must be .9999 fine or US Eagles
- ❑ Silver Bullion coins and bars must be .999 fine
- ❑ U.S. Treasury Gold and Silver Coins
- ❑ Small business start ups
- ❑ Tax Lien Certificates
- ❑ Trust Deeds
- ❑ Mortgage Notes
- ❑ Single and Multi Family Residential Property
- ❑ Securities
- ❑ CD's
- ❑ Stocks
- ❑ Bonds
- ❑ Mutual Funds
- ❑ LLC's
- ❑ Apartment Buildings
- ❑ Co-Ops
- ❑ Condominiums
- ❑ Commercial Property
- ❑ Joint Ventures
- ❑ Improved or Unimproved Land
- ❑ Commodities
- ❑ Futures
- ❑ Contracts of Sale
- ❑ Factoring
- ❑ Like and Unlike Exchanges
- ❑ Leases
- ❑ Palladium
- ❑ Life Insurance

LIFE INSURANCE

Life insurance can be purchased within a QRP. Life Insurance is not allowed in an IRA. Life insurance must be "incidental" to the main retirement purpose of the plan, so there are limits on the amount of life insurance that can be purchased on behalf of a plan participant. These rules are different for defined benefit plans and defined contribution plans. Under a defined benefit plan, the face amount of insurance generally cannot exceed 100 times the participant's projected monthly retirement benefit.

Example: If the projected monthly retirement benefit were $4,000, the limit on the life insurance that could be provided would be $400,000. Coverage in excess of this amount would not be deemed "incidental."

http://www.eegroup.com/life_ins_in_qual_plan.html

WHO MAY BE INVOLVED IN YOUR INVESTMENT DECISION

The following may be involved with your transaction along with you:

- ❑ Participants in the Qualified Plan
- ❑ Accountant
- ❑ Attorney or Escrow Agent
- ❑ Financial Advisor
- ❑ Lender(s)
- ❑ Partners
- ❑ Seller
- ❑ Trustee or Custodian and/or Administrator/Record Keeper

DISALLOWED ASSETS:

Anything considered a collectible, such as:

- x   Art
- x   Rugs
- x   Stamp or Collectible Coins (certain bullion coins are allowed, as specified above)
- x   Metal or Gem
- x   Antiques

REAL ESTATE

You can invest and hold almost any type of real estate you'd like with your QRP other then a property that you or a disqualified party receive any current benefit from.

For Example you can buy a vacation house in San Diego to rent out but you can't use it one weekend a year and then rent it out the rest of the time. This would be considered receiving a current benefit from it.

The IRS does not permit active investments inside a qualified plan. This means you can't buy a property, spend a bunch of time fixing it up and then selling it and deferring the gains and income inside your plan. The IRS looks at that type of activity and calls it a business or trade and imposes a 35% tax through UBIT (Unrelated Business Income Tax). We've heard of people getting away with doing this, adding a little bit of work here and there but we encourage you to play by the rules. See *Internal Revenue Code § 4975*

If you buy a property stick with those that are professionally managed. The truth is that the property should be able to support professional property management anyway. If it can't survive

financially without you doing all the work, you may want to rethink investing in it in the first place.

If you do want to buy a property and do the work yourself, consider doing the investment inside a corporation or LLC enjoying the tax advantages there, not risking the violation of running an active business inside a qualified plan.

The law allows you to contribute a certain amount of money to your plan each year, lets say that amount is $18,000. If you spent 500 hours doing labor doing work to the property you're really contributing another $5000, $10,000 or more depending on what that labor time would have cost on the open market. You've effectively back-door contributed to your plan above the limits the government set. We don't recommend doing this.

A QRP is allowed to take out debt, called qualified debt, to purchase a property but the debt is required to be non-recourse, meaning neither you nor the QRP can guarantee it. The property is the only thing that can be used for collateral or as a guarantee. You generally do not have limits on the amount of debt relative to the property and will not have problems with UDFI (unrelated debt financed income) or UBIT, (unrelated business income tax) when you use debt on property inside your QRP.

Unfortunately IRA's are not exempt from UDFI and profits from an investment using debt that an IRA makes would be forced to pay the penalty. Any real estate investor should think twice before investing their retirement money in real estate with debt because of the penalty.

For this reason alone the QRP is vastly superior to the IRA for a real estate investor.

PRECIOUS METALS—GOLD, SILVER & PLATINUM

The QRP is unique in it's ability for an owner of the plan or anyone else to be trustee and manage account assets. (see: USC § 403b) This includes deciding on the facility to store precious metals so long as they are managed with reasonable care and no disqualified party receives current benefit. (see ERISA 29 USC § 1103) You couldn't receive the bullion and turn it into jewelry for example. This would be considered receiving a current benefit.

As a trustee you are in a fiduciary role to protect the assets so if your plan buys gold you'd be violating your responsibilities as a fiduciary if you buried the assets in your back yard.

Holding the assets of the plan in a bank safety deposit box or in a vault at home is reasonable and should cause no problems with the IRS or Department of Labor in terms of custody and care of assets.

> **WARNING: IRA's are vastly different than the QRP because USC § 408 requires an IRA custodian of assets to be a bank or non-bank custodian. A non-bank custodian must seek approval by the IRS. Any type of self directed IRA that suggest you can avoid this custodian requirement by setting up a shell company that takes ownership of metals is likely jeopardizing the assets of the IRA should the IRS find out. This is a case of the form of the structure satisfies the USC § 408 but the substance of the structure does not and is therefore a violation in the Department of Labor and IRS' eyes.**

The following gold, silver, platinum and palladium are permissible. There may be more but these clearly fall into the permissible category given the IRS and DOL guidelines as of 2012

❑ Acceptable Gold Coins (31 USC § 5112):

- US Minted Eagles of any size
- US Minted Buffalos
- Austrian Philharmonic Coins, Australian Kangaroo and Nuggets, Kookaburras and Koala Coins
- Canadian Maple Leaf Coins, any size

❑ Gold bars and rounds manufactured by a NYMEX or COMEX approved refiner/assayer and meeting minimum fineness requirements of .995+; most gold bullion bars are 99.99% pure, what the industry calls "four 9s gold." as described in section 7 of the Commodity Exchange Act, 7 USC 7

- Investors with large QRP's should consider the ten-ounce and the kilo bars (32.15 ounces) because the larger bars carry smaller markups over spot. As a rule, the larger the bar, the smaller the markup

❑ Acceptable Silver Coins (31 USC § 5112):

- US Minted Eagles
- Canadian Maple Leafs
- Silver Mexican Libertads
- Silver bars and rounds manufactured by a COMEX approved refiner/assayer and meeting minimum fineness requirements of .999+ as described in section 7 of the Commodity Exchange Act, 7 USC 7

❑ Acceptable Platinum

- Canadian Maple Leafs
- Platinum bars and rounds manufactured by a NYMEX approved refiner/assayer and meeting minimum

fineness requirements of .9995+, as described in section 7 of the Commodity Exchange Act, 7 USC 7

❑ Acceptable Palladium

- Canadian Maple Leafs
- Platinum Isle of Man Noble Coins
- Palladium bars and rounds manufactured by a NYMEX approved refiner/assayer and meeting minimum fineness requirements of .9995+, as described in section 7 of the Commodity Exchange Act, 7 USC 7

Disallowed Investments & Prohibited Transactions

DISALLOWED INVESTMENTS

Collectibles

For purposes of this subsection, the term "collectible" means:

- ❑ Any work of art
- ❑ Any rug or antique or autos
- ❑ Any metal or gem
- ❑ Any stamp or coin
- ❑ Any other tangible personal property specified by the Secretary of the Department of Labor for purposes of this subsection

PROHIBITED TRANSACTIONS

A prohibited transaction is any improper or illegal use of a qualified plan by the plan participant or any disqualified person. If you or your beneficiary engages in a prohibited transaction (as defined under Section 4975 of the Internal Revenue Code), the plan **could lose its tax exemption** and you must include the value of your account in your gross income for that taxable year.

You are a disqualified person if you are:

- ❑ An employer of any of the participants in the plan
- ❑ A 10% (or greater) partner in a partnership that has the plan
- ❑ A fiduciary of the plan (including yourself and any advisors)
- ❑ A highly compensated partner (an employee who makes 10% or more of the employer's annual wages)

- ❑ An employee organization with any participating members who are covered by the plan
- ❑ A person providing services to the plan
- ❑ If you are a disqualified person, your related persons will also be disqualified persons. These related persons include members of the plan owner's family such as:

  - Spouses, ancestors, direct descendants and any spouses of direct descendants
  - Corporations, partnerships, trusts or estates in which you own, directly or indirectly, at least half of the total voting stock or the value of all stock of a corporation, beneficial interest of the trust or estate
  - Capital interest or profit interest in the partnership

PROHIBITED TRANSACTIONS BETWEEN DISQUALIFIED PERSONS:

- ❑ A transfer of plan income or assets to, or use of plan income or assets by, or for the benefit of, a disqualified person, is a prohibited transaction.
- ❑ Dealing with plan income or assets by a fiduciary for his or her own interest is a prohibited transaction.
- ❑ The receiving of consideration by a fiduciary for his or her own account from a party that is dealing with the plan in a transaction that involves plan income or assets is prohibited transaction.

Prohibited Transactions between the plan and disqualified person:

- ❑ Selling, exchanging or leasing property
- ❑ Lending money or extending credit
- ❑ Furnishing goods, services or facilities

AVOIDING PROHIBITED TRANSACTIONS

The following are acts that you should avoid:

- ❏ Improper use of your Qualified Plan Assets by you or any disqualified person
- ❏ Borrowing money from it and not following prescribed regulations
- ❏ Selling property to it
- ❏ Using it as security for a loan

EXEMPTIONS

A prohibited transaction does not take place if you are a disqualified person and receive any benefit to which you are entitled to as a plan participant or beneficiary. However, the benefit must be calculated and paid under the same terms as all other participants and beneficiaries.

The same transaction involving a 401(k) plan

The purchase of a property in a 401(k) Plan is as straightforward as making the purchases personally. The only difference is that there is an intermediary, such as a trustee or a Third Party Administrator (TPA) performing the transaction on behalf of your Profit Sharing 401(k) Plan. In most cases this person is you.

Unrelated business income tax on debt financed property involving a qualified plan

In many circumstances, UDFI does not apply to income from debt financed property in a qualified plan. There is a limited exception in the definition of acquisition indebtedness contained in section

514(c) (9) of the Internal Revenue Code for plans under section 401, including profit sharing, 401(k) plan, and defined benefit plans. For more information on this exemption, please see your tax advisor.

Establishing a QRP

The first step in setting up a qualified retirement plan is to establish a written plan, which fulfills the requirements of the IRS. The written plan must be adopted by the last day of the tax year in which the employer starts the plan. The employer is then required to communicate the specifics of the plan to eligible employees. The basic steps in setting up a qualified retirement plan are easy and usually take less then 3 business days.

1. Fill out the 1 page information sheet at *www.TheQRP.org* and submit on-line or 800. 270.1649
2. Our office will then prepare the complete set of plan documents and mail them to your address for signature. We will also include your new **Federal Identification Number** to set up your new bank or a brokerage account.
3. Sign the 2 sets of signature pages (your complete copy in the binder and our office file copy signature pages) and return the signature pages to us via mail in the envelope provide with your documents.
4. Inform employees of the plan specifics
5. Take the plan documents and Federal ID# to any financial institution and open up your bank accounts.
6. Request your IRA's and 401(k)'s are rolled over tax free.
7. You can now make plan contributions.
8. Invest the plan assets.

QRP Administration

In addition to the requirements for establishing a qualified retirement plan, you are responsible for operating the plan. After the QRP is established, you are responsible for operational and administrative duties. These administrative responsibilities include:

Making contributions in accordance with the plan.

❑ Keeping the plan up-to-date and in compliance with all retirement plan laws.
❑ Investing the plan assets.
❑ Providing information and required disclosure to plan participants.
❑ Distributing benefits in accordance with the plan.
❑ Informing eligible employees about in the plan.

INFORMATION RETURNS

Form 5500-EZ, *Annual Return of One-Participant (Owners and Their Spouses) Retirement Plan*, is a short-form information return that is filed by pension plans, profit-sharing plans, and 401(k) plans that cover:

❑ Only owners or an individual and his or her spouse who wholly own the trade or business for which the plan is established.
❑ Only partners and their spouses in a business partnership for which the plan is established.

Form 5500-EZ must be filed annually. If your plan has $250,000 in assets or more OR you hire employees that are part of the plan. According to the instructions for both Form 5500 and 5500-EZ, each form is due by the last day of the seventh calendar month after the end of the plan year.

Savers Credit

Couples get up to $2,000 FREE from the U.S. government

You are entitled to a tax credit of up to 50% of your contribution (up to $1,000) to nearly any type of retirement plan. For individuals with incomes under $55,000, a retirement savings contribution credit is provided in the tax laws and provides up to a $2,000 nonrefundable "saver's credit" to encourage contributions to certain types of retirement plans, such as 401(k)s and Profit Sharing Plans. The amount of the credit is based upon the total contributions to qualified retirement plans plus elective deferrals. The credit rate can be as low as 10% or as high as 50% (IRS publication 560).

Tax Alerts

Penalties for Failure to Report or Disclose

P lan administrators, employers, and other parties are liable for penalties for failing to comply with reporting and disclosure rules. The IRS imposes a penalty of $25 per day (up to $15,000) for not filing returns in connection with pension, profit-sharing, and other retirement plans by the required due date.

The Department Of Labor may assess a civil penalty of up to $1,100 per day against a plan administrator from the date of the administrator's failure or refusal to file an annual report until the report is filed.

What are the advantages of a Qualified Retirement Plan over an IRA?

	Qualified Plan	**IRA**
Can you borrow from you retirement account?	YES- Permitted up to $50,000 or ½ vested account	Not Allowed
Debt financing on real estate without adverse tax consequences?	Permitted	Not permitted
Deductible contribution limit for 2017?	$54,000 for 401(k)	Only $5,500
Protection from creditors in lawsuits?	YES-ERISA provided protection	No-ERISA protection
Protection from creditors in Bankruptcy?	YES-ERISA provided protection	Minimal and subjective

Ability to purchase life insurance?	YES	Not permitted
Ability to be your own trustee, write and sign checks, and directly control your plan assets?	YES	Not permitted
Employee contribution (elective deferrals)	$18,000	Not Permitted
Catch up contributions if over age 50	$ 6,000	$1,000

The 8ᵗʰ Wonder of the World

Compound interest is the eighth wonder of the world. He who understands it, earns it ... he who doesn't ... pays it.

—Albert Einstein

The inverse of that is taxation, possibly the most destructive force on wealth ever.

Saving cash, you get taxed each year for the money as it comes out of your paycheck, and all the interest earned on that money. Tax deferral, or QRP, takes the money out to your paycheck pre-tax, you are not taxed as the money grows in the account, then you are taxed when the money is taken out for all the money that is taken out (principal and interest are taxed the same). Tax Avoidance, or ROTH QRP is paying the taxes up front for the principal amount, but the interest earned is never taxed. In the tax avoidance situation, the only tax paid is that on your income at the same rate as all other taxable income.

To illustrate the power of taxation vs. tax deferral vs. tax avoidance here are a few scenarios. Since we are only looking at how tax effects your situation, we will have the same salary and contribution rates for each scenario.:

This scenario assumes your tax rate will remain the same throughout the 30 years that you are going to work and contribute, as well as assuming that you will contribute the maximum allotted funds each year.

Scenario #1

Income: $150,000
Income tax rate today 35%
Income tax rate at retirement 35%
Assumed Interest Rate (based on Tax Lien Investments): 16%
Annual Contribution or Earnings to use for investing $18,000

30-year period of earnings and investments:

Cash (No tax strategy) vs. QRP vs. ROTH QRP

In 30 years the net result is:

Cash strategy: $2.34mil
QRP: $7.00 mil
ROTH QRP: $7.52mil

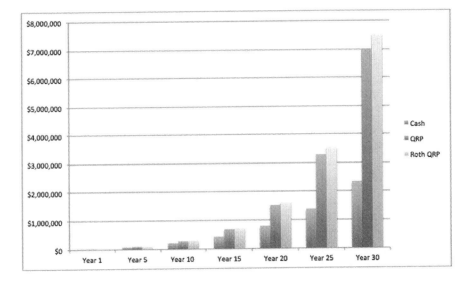

Scenario #2

Income tax rate today 35%

Income tax rate at retirement 50% (assumes tax rate of 35% in years 1-24)

Annual Contribution or Earnings to use for investing $18,000

30-year period of earnings and investments:

No tax strategy vs. QRP vs. ROTH QRP

In 30 years the net result is:

Cash strategy: $2.29 mil
QRP: $5.38 mil
ROTH QRP: $7.52 mil

Section 2

QRP vs. et.al

What are the advantages of a QRP vs. an IRA?

❑ With a QRP, you can be the trustee which means you make all the investment decision, write/sign checks, and have full control of the plan. You cannot be the trustee of an IRA.

IRS Publication 590 clearly states the following in regards to an IRA:

> *"An individual retirement account (IRA) is a trust or custodial account set up in the United States for the exclusive benefit of you or your beneficiaries. The account is created by a written document. The document must show that the account meets all of the following requirements. The trustee or custodian must be a bank, a federally insured credit union, a savings and loan association, or an entity approved by the IRS to act as trustee or custodian…"*

—Source: *IRS Publication 590*

❑ You can borrow money from your QRP. You can borrow up to $50,000 or ½ your vested account balance, whichever is less, from your QRP. You cannot borrow from an IRA.
❑ Under ERISA laws, a QRP has protection from creditors, IRS, and bankruptcy. An IRA is not protected from creditors, IRS, or bankruptcy.
❑ Contribution limit for a QRP in 2017 is $54,000 ($18,000 individual + corporate contributions) annually. You can only contribute $5,500 annually to an IRA.
❑ A QRP allows you to purchase life insurance. You cannot purchase life insurance with an IRA.

EXHIBIT 1

Comparison of Plan Types and Uses— Tax-Deferred and Tax-Free Investing (2013)

OBJECTIVES IN A TAX-DEFERRED PLAN?	QRP	IRA
As an employer, do you want to be able to contribute up to 25% of compensation for a given year?	YES To a maximum of $53,000	Maximum by law
As an employee, do you want to defer up to 100% of compensation?	Yes To a maximum of $18,000 plus catch-up provision of $6,000 (Not counted as part of the 25% of your employer contribution)	Not Applicable
Do you want to self-direct all of your investments?	YES	YES – but most use a 3rd party
Do you want to be your own Trustee, Custodian and Administrator? For Example: Write and sign checks, sign all documents and /or take possession of Plan assets for; your account?	YES, or you may appoint others for each of these roles	Not Permitted by Law
Do you want to borrow from your Retirement Account?	YES, Up to a maximum of $50,000 of your vested Account Balance	Not Permitted by Law
Do you want to retire before age 59 ½ and receive distributions penalty free?	YES, age 55 is an acceptable retirement age	59 ½ is the earliest, without substantially equal periodic payments

Do you want to make sure that your assets are protected from creditors?	YES, Your benefits are not accessible to creditors, as ERISA provided for your benefits to be "Non-alienable"	No anti-alienation provision exists, but many states protect a portion of assets
Do you want Life Insurance as part of your retirement portfolio?	YES	Prohibited
Do you want to be able to make "in kind" contributions of assets that you own, not just cash?	YES, provided that you have no common law employees, and the Plan covers you, your spouse and partners only.	Not Permitted

Note: self-employed individuals take into account the deductions allowed for one-half of the self-employment tax and contributions to the plan.

EXHIBIT 2

Advantages of a Qualified Retirement Plan (QRP) Vs. an IRA

	IRA's	QRP
Custodians	☐ You are Required to have a bank or trust company serve as the custodian	☑ No Custodian Required - Self-Trustee Allowed
Nationalization / Confiscation	☐ Vulnerable to both	☑ PROTECTED
Flexibility in form	☐ No, all IRA's are the same	☑ Yes, massive flexibility and expansion options, they vary according to the trust documents and are very specific
Document Size	☐ Simple, short document	☑ Extensive plan docs 100's of pages
Protection from Creditors		
Judgement Proof	☐ Limited	☑ Yes
Survives Bankruptcy	☐ Limited	☑ Yes
Covered by ERISA?	☐ NO	☑ Yes
Investing Options & borrowing		
Can I take a loan out against the assets?	☐ NO	☑ YES - Up to $50,000
Operations		
Checkbook control	Requires setting up an LLC	No LLC Required for Checkbook Control
Control & Fees		
Owner gets CONTROL	☐ NO	☑ Yes
Annual fees	lots of maintenance and transaction fees	No Custodian Fees
Owners can Physically Hold Gold & Silver	☐ NO	☑ Yes
Can I use debt to finance Real Estate and avoid UDFI (Unrelated Debt-financed Income) tax?	☐ NO	☑ Yes
Contributions		
Annual Maximum Contribution per person 2016	$5,500	$53,000
Income Limits?	Yes	No
Catch up contributions over age 50	$1,000	$6,000
Tax Credits?		
Do I get any Tax Credits & deductions for setting this up?	NONE	☑ Yes - $1500
Ability to buy life insurance	☐ NO	☑ Yes

Section 3

The Special ROLLOVER QRP

To be eligible to benefit from the Rollover QRP you must meet one of these two tests plus have intent to generate revenue:

1. You have a qualified account (a 401k, 403b or 457) from a previous employer that you no longer work for or an IRA with qualified money
2. A qualified account with a current employer that has an "In-Service" option in the plan allowing you to roll over your retirement funds while still working for the employer (you're considered still in-service for the employer but are allowed to distribute)

Do you have a 401k, 403b or 457 account from a previous employer? Your retirement money may still be with the previous plans administrator or you may have rolled it into an IRA. (an IRA that was created from doing a rollover of a 401k, 403b or 457 is called a Conduit IRA)

What you want:

You want to invest your retirement account in alternative investments like gold, silver, real estate, private lending etc. instead of the typical "faulty five" pack offered by many employers' 401k.

The faulty five often look like a selection of investments:

- ❏ Money Market Fund
- ❏ Bond Fund
- ❏ Small Cap Stock Fund
- ❏ Big Cap Stock Fund
- ❏ International Fund

What you really want is the ability to invest in assets like:

- ❏ Gold and Silver Bars and coins
- ❏ Real Estate, domestic and international
- ❏ Land
- ❏ Commercial paper, including mortgages
- ❏ Private businesses
- ❏ Stocks, Bonds and Mutual funds
- ❏ Foreign Currencies
- ❏ Private placements
- ❏ Tax liens

With your Rollover QRP you can invest in all these things and more. The IRS only disallows certain things as investments and certain persons from being a part of the transaction.

Disallowed Investments and Disqualified Persons

The Internal Revenue Code does not describe what a QRP can invest in, only what it cannot invest in. Internal Revenue Code Section 4975 prohibits Disqualified Persons from engaging in certain type of transactions. The purpose of these rules is to encourage the use of retirement funds for accumulation and prohibit those in control of retirement funds from taking advantage of the tax benefits for their personal account. For a full list of disallowed items and the definition of a Disqualified Person, see this section (In the Definitions section)

1. **Set up a QRP**: fill out the form online and submit the information, about 2 weeks later you'll receive your trust docs. Review them and you're ready to fund:

2. **Set up a Bank Account**: Take your QRP papers to any bank you like and set up a checking account for the QRP

3. **Fund the QRP.** Ask your current custodian to transfer funds from your old plan to your QRP. Any qualified account that can be rolled over into the QRP is done tax free and penalty free in every case.

4. **Invest.** Invest in whatever you'd like: as long as you're investing in an allowed investment and not something disqualified or with a disqualified person you can write the check for the investment.

5. **Management**: Keep up with the bookkeeping on anything your QRP does. The IRS requires basic record keeping. You can also hire a bookkeeper, accountant or third party to do this very inexpensively.

Section 4

The Real Estate Investor QRP

A Real Estate Investor (REI QRP) QRP aka a solo 401(k) is designed for the self-employed or small business owner with no other employees or a small number of employees. It offers powerful features not found in traditional 401(k) or IRA retirement plans.

> To be eligible to benefit from the REI QRP you must meet two tests:
>
> ✓ The presence of some type of self employment activity (Real Estate investing)
> ✓ The absence of full-time employees other then you and/or your spouse.

The Presence of Self-Employment Activity

Self Employment activity generally includes ownership and operation of a Sole Proprietorship, Limited Liability Company (LLC), C Corporation, S Corporation or a Limited Partnership where the business intends to generate revenue for profit and make contributions to the plan. Once the company is created, there must be income based on the work of those entities to contribute to the retirement plan. Any contributions must be derived from earned income reported on a W-2 subject to self-employment tax.

Generating Revenue for Profit

There are no established thresholds for how much profit the business must generate, how much money must be contributed to the plan, or how soon profits and contributions must happen. It's generally believed that the IRS will consider the business eligible if it is conducting legitimate business that is run with the intention of generating profits. The self-employment activity can be part time and it can be ancillary to the owners full or part time employment elsewhere.

Checkbook Control

A REI QRP allows you, the owner, to choose any person you'd like to be the trustee, including yourself. The trustee is responsible for writing checks for investments. This is where **Checkbook Control** comes from. As trustee of the plan, you no longer have to get each and every investment you'd like to make approved by an outside custodian or trustee. If you want to invest it's as simple writing a check.

This control means all assets of the QRP trust are under your sole authority. It also means you eliminate the expense and delays associated with a custodian like you're required to have with an IRA. This enables you to act quickly when the right investment presents itself to you.

> USC §408 requires all IRA's to have a bank or approved non-bank custodian. IRA's are not allowed to ignore this requirement through tricky maneuvers like the IRA LLC that promoters claim gets around this requirement. Just because some people may be getting away with this rule doesn't mean the activity is allowed. Be warned, this is a dangerous game to play and the penalty is up to 115% of assets that are part of any scheme to violate the rules or that involve prohibited transactions.

Administration, Maintenance and Compliance

Operating the QRP is as simple as writing checks and keeping a basic accounting of what the plan has invested in, expenses of the plan and any revenue the plan earns. Most of the administration is keeping good records of investment activities, receipts and statements. Once the plan has more then $250,000 in assets you're required to file a short form with the IRS, (Form 5500EZ can be filed online if you have less then $250,000 in assets in the plan).

Rollover Options

You are permitted to rollover any investment money from a previous employer's 401(k), 403b or 457 or other qualified money like from an IRA or SEP. You're allowed to transfer those funds and assets into your RE QRP. If you previously rolled over a 401k, 403b or 457 into an IRA you can do another rollover from the IRA into your QRP. This type of IRA is classified as a **Conduit IRA**. All of these types of rollovers should be tax free and penalty free.

Make sure you transfer the funds directly from the trustee to trustee in order to avoid the 20% withholding requirement.

You can roll over as many different accounts as you'd like and consolidate them into your QRP as long as they're qualified accounts like 401k, 403b, 457's, IRA's etc. Consolidating all these funds should save you money and time managing the funds and investing. It's a good idea to keep these funds in different checking accounts once you roll them into your QRP. Please call us for further details about the various structures that might necessitate separate checking accounts.

The Roth Option:

In all the examples above the employee deferral contributions can be pretax or can be a Roth type contribution (contributed with after tax money). The profit sharing employer contribution must be made as a pre-tax contribution.

The Loan

With a QRP you're permitted to borrow money from your plan for any purpose at any time. Pursuant to Internal Revenue Code Section 72(p), a Solo QRP loan is permitted at any time using the accumulated balance of the QRP as collateral for the loan. A Solo QRP participant can borrow up to either $50,000 or 50% of their account value-whichever is less. The loan must be repaid within 5 years and fully amortized within the chosen period of time with equal payments, no less then quarterly. The IRS requires a reasonable interest rate which generally means prime plus 1%. Prime in 2012 was around 3% so a minimum safe rate would be around 4%. Of course if you paid a higher amount this would be one legal strategy to get more money into your plan in addition to the annual contributions.

Internal Revenue Code Section 72(p) and the 2001 EGTRRA law established the framework for a Solo QRP participant to borrow money from his QRP account. As long as the plan documents allow for it and the proper loan documents are prepared and executed, a participant can borrow money for his or her Solo QRP account for any purpose. The Solo QRP loan is received tax-free and penalty-free. There are no penalties or taxes due provided the loan payments are paid on time. The QRP documents you receive from QRP Associates allow you to borrow money from your Solo QRP for any purpose, including real estate, funding your own business, paying off personal debt, going on vacation, etc.

The Ultimate Emergency Fund

Ever since the meltdown in 2008 banks have become more and more rigid about lending and have almost completely cut off lending to small businesses. The Total Control QRP is a perfect structure for any self-employed business owner seeking immediate funds for their business without having to beg the bank.

Investment Options

A QRP plan allows you to invest in almost any type of investment you can think of other then the small list of disallowed items and disqualified persons. Any income and gains from an investment are required to go directly back to your QRP plan and flow back tax free.

Some of the options you may choose to invest in are:

- ❑ Gold and Silver Bars and coins* (see the metals supplement)
- ❑ Real Estate, domestic and international
- ❑ Land
- ❑ Commercial paper, including mortgages
- ❑ Private businesses
- ❑ Stocks, Bonds and Mutual funds
- ❑ Foreign Currencies
- ❑ Private placements
- ❑ Tax liens

Disallowed Investments and Disqualified Persons

The Internal Revenue Code does not describe what a QRP can invest in, only what it cannot invest in. Internal Revenue Code Section 4975 prohibits Disqualified Persons from engaging in certain type of transactions. The purpose of these rules is to encourage the use of retirement funds for accumulation and prohibit those in control of retirement funds from taking advantage of the tax benefits for their personal account. For a full list of disallowed items and the definition of a Disqualified Person, see the section on DI's and DP's.

EGTRRA—Clarifying the QRP for a self employed person

In 2001, the Economic Growth and Tax Relief Reconciliation Act (EGTRRA) was passed. This act clarified how a QRP could be used by a self employed person who has no full time employees. It also clarified that the self-employed QRP participant can make contributions as both employee via elective deferral and employer via profit sharing. This dual contribution results in substantially higher limits then an IRA or other common vehicles.

Summary

The Real Estate Investors QRP is a highly flexible and tax-efficient retirement solution that will allow you to make high contributions to the plan either pre-tax or by designating it a ROTH and building part of it 100% tax free.

- ❑ Contribute up to $53,000 a year ($59,000 if you're over 50)
- ❑ Borrow up to $50,000 or 50% of your account value (whichever is less)
- ❑ Invest in almost any type of investment tax free including:
- ❑ Precious metals like Gold, Silver and Platinum
- ❑ Real estate
- ❑ Tax liens
- ❑ Private businesses
- ❑ Private loans
- ❑ Wall Street stuff like stocks and bonds

With a solo QRP you're able to use your retirement funds to make almost any type of investment on your own without requiring the "consent" of anyone else like a custodian. The last thing you want is some technical bureaucrat telling you what you can or can't do with your own money, especially when the IRS has been very specific about what the rules are. Why would you limit your choices by working with a custodian? Plus, you have to pay fees to this person for the service of telling you no!!!

As a trustee of the REI QRP, you will have "Checkbook Control" over the QRP assets.

The REI QRP allows you to invest tax free in an investment that you know and understand and even allows you to borrow up to $50,000 or 50% of the account for any purpose.

Aside from certain "prohibited transactions" involving Disqualified Persons, which are outlined in the Internal Revenue Code Section 4975, a QRP can invest in most of the commonly made investments, including real estate, private business entities, public and private shares in companies and commercial and private paper.

Self-employed individuals: You can make contributions on behalf of yourself only if you have net earnings (Compensation) from self-employment in the trade or business for which the plan was set up. Your net earnings must be from your personal services, not from your investments. If you have a net loss from self-employment, you cannot make contributions for yourself for the year, even if you can contribute for common-law employees based on their compensation.

What if you have a job that offers a 401k or other retirement plan?

You can participate in an employers 401(k) plan in tandem with your own Solo QRP. In that case the employee-elective deferrals from both plans are subject to the single contribution limit. ($18,000 in 2017 or $24,000 if over age 50) The maximum elective deferral contribution you can make as an employee, is $18,000 regardless of how many retirement plans you are involved in.

Section 5

The QRP Dictionary

401 (k): A qualified retirement savings plan that allows employees to set aside tax- deferred income for retirement. In 2017, an employee can contribute up to $18,000 annually if they're under 50 or $24,000 if they're age 50 or over. A 401(k) is truly self-directed, allowing participants to invest in both traditional and non-traditional assets. Companies have the option to make matching contributions. This is a defined contribution plan. There are various 401(k) options: Roth, Traditional, Self- directed, and Profit Sharing options.

A

Active Income: Income you are earning through actions performed for a company. This is any income based on employment and subject to social security and other taxes.

Annual Additions: The total of all an employee's contributions for a year. This does not include roll- over money from other accounts or previous years

Annual Benefits: What the employee receives yearly on an annuity basis. The benefits are the money taken out of the account (distribution), and they are taken on once every year.

Annuity: A specific amount of money received for a specific amount of time. For Example: Johnny gets $50,000/ year for 25 years. If Johnny dies the payments stop. There is no getting more or less money out, and usually there is no transferring the benefit. The amount received is the annual benefit.

B

Beneficiary: Person who receives the funds from the retirement plan. Just as the "benefit" is the money taken out, the beneficiary is the person who receives the money.

Business: A business is an activity in which a profit motive is present and economic activity is involved. Required to set up a QRP.

C

Catch-up contribution: Additional employee contributions that can be made only by those who attain age 50 by the end of the year. This is what allows participants over 50 years old to add more into their retirement plans . . . so they can "catch up" to what a younger person would be able to contribute.

Cliff Vesting: This is when an employee is 100% vested on a given date. That date, is the cliff that the employee has reached. For Example, a company says that an employee has full access to all the money that the company has put into their account (vested) when the employee has worked there for 2 years. In this example, the employee has no access to the money that the company put into the retirement account, until they have worked for that company for 2 years.

Collectible Items (as defined by the IRS): These are the items that are not allowed to be purchased with a retirement account:

- ❏ Any work of art,
- ❏ Any rug or antique,
- ❏ Any metal or gem,
- ❏ Any stamp or coin,

- Acceptable Gold Coins (can be purchased with retirement accounts):

  ✓ A fifty dollar gold coin that is 32.7 millimeters in diameter, weighs 33.931 grams, and contains **one troy ounce of fine gold.**

  ✓ A twenty-five dollar gold coin that is 27.0 millimeters in diameter, weighs 16.966 grams, and contains **one-half troy ounce of fine gold.**

  ✓ A ten dollar gold coin that is 22.0 millimeters in diameter, weighs 8.483 grams, and contains **one-fourth troy ounce of fine gold.**

  ✓ A five dollar gold coin that is 16.5 millimeters in diameter, weighs 3.393 grams, and contains **one-tenth troy ounce of fine gold.**

- Acceptable Silver Coins (can be purchased with retirement accounts):

  ✓ are 40.6 millimeters in diameter and weigh 31.103 grams;

  ✓ contain .999 fine silver;

  ✓ have a design—

  ✓ symbolic of Liberty on the obverse side; and

  ✓ of an eagle on the reverse side;

  ✓ have inscriptions of the year of minting or issuance, and the words "Liberty," "In God We Trust," "United States of America," "1 Oz. Fine Silver," "E Pluribus Unum," and "One Dollar,"; and

  ✓ have reeded edges.

Common Law Employee: Any person under common law would be considered an employee. For example, if the employer provides the employee's tools, materials, and workplace, and the employer can fire them person, they are a common- law employee.

Common Law employees are not self- employed and can not set up retirement plan for themselves.

Compensation: All the payments an employee receives, including wages and salaries, fees for professional services, commissions and tips, fringe benefits, and bonuses. Compensation also includes any elective deferrals. Compensation does not include nontaxable reimbursement, like expenses or non-elective deferrals.

Conduit IRA: An IRA that was funded with a rolled over 401(k), or other qualified retirement plan, such as 403b or 457.

Contribution Deadline: The last moment someone can add money to their retirement plan that year. For a qualified plan, this can actually be after the tax return is completed, and the return can be used to fund the account for the same year. You can make deductible contributions for a tax year up to the due date of your return (plus extensions) for that year. You can make contributions on behalf of yourself only if you have net earnings (Compensation) from self-employment in the trade or business for which the plan was set up. Your net earnings must be from your personal services, not from your investments. If you have a net loss from self-employment, you cannot make contributions for yourself for the year, even if you can contribute for common-law employees based on their compensation.

You generally apply your plan contributions to the year in which you make them. But you can apply them to the previous year if all the following requirements are met.

- ❏ You make them by the due date of your tax return for the previous year (including extensions).
- ❏ The plan was established by the end of the previous year.
- ❏ The plan treats the contributions as though it had received them on the last day of the previous year.

Contribution Limits: The amount that an employee or employer can no longer receive tax benefits for. So, you can put as much money as you want into a retirement account, but after a certain dollar amount, you no longer receive the tax benefits from those contributions. There is no penalty for taking that extra money out of the account, if the contributor goes over the limit.

Coverage: Qualified plans must include a certain percentage of rank-and-file employees.

D

Deadline to Contribute—see Contribution deadline

Defined Benefit Plan: This is essentially a pension. This account has a set amount that the beneficiary will receive at retirement. Because the end result is set, contributions change based on how the account is performing. Not knowing how the investments will perform, means the employee, and the employer are less able to prepare and plan on their contributions, because the goal is set, not the contribution. These are great for CEO's and those who want to contribute significantly more money to their retirement.

Defined Contribution Plan: These are individual plans, and the outcome, the result, the amount you get at retirement is based on how much the employee puts in (contributes) and how the investments perform. So, this means the plan is defined, or run by the contributions that are put into the accounts. These are the IRA's, 401(k)'s, profit sharing plans, etc. So, there are some Defined Contribution Plans that are Qualified Retirement Plans, and some that are Unqualified.

Disqualified Persons: The IRS has determined that there are some people the participant is not allowed to purchase things from when using their qualified retirement plan. Congress did this to prevent certain parties from doing suspicious or fraudulent deals. *See FAQ's under Disqualified Persons*

Disallowed Investments: A few things that a qualified retirement plan cannot be used to purchase or fund.

E

Early Distribution: Anytime you take money out of your retirement plan before age 59.5 is early. For most early distributions the participant must pay a 10% penalty, plus the tax penalty (which is at the rate of income tax) for the distribution. There are a few exceptions that allow you to bypass the 10% penalties, but the participant will still pay the income tax. If the participant dies, their beneficiary has immediate access to their account. If the participant is disabled, there is no penalty for the early distribution. If the participant sets it up as annuity for the rest of their life expectancy, then there is no 10% penalty (this helps the government, they are guaranteed monthly tax distribution, so they allow it). A few other exemptions are: if you leave your company after age 55; you need it to pay your child support; if you put more into the account than you are allowed to deduct from your taxes, you can take out the excess; medical expenses; or mandatory distributions (you are 70.5 years old, but not retired).

Earned Income: Net earnings from self-employment, from a business that you directly impacted with your work. This would also include any royalties from a book or invention. Earnings from personal effort or labor are subject to self employment tax, including social security tax.

Elective Deferral: The amount of pre-tax salary that the employee chooses to put into a retirement plan. This only applies to accounts that use pre-tax dollars, like the 401(k). A Roth 401(k) would use after tax dollars.

Your qualified plan can include a cash or deferred arrangement under which participants can choose to have you contribute part of their before – tax compensation to the plan rather then receive the compensation in cash. A plan with this type of arrangement is popularly know as a "401k plan." (As a self-employed individual participating in the plan, you can contribute part of your before-tax net earnings from the business). This contribution is called an "elective" deferral" because participants choose (elect) to defer receipt of the money. In general, a qualified plan can include a cash or deferred arrangement only if the qualified plan is one of the following:

- ❏ A Profit sharing plan
- ❏ Matching contributions. If your plan permits you can make matching contributions for an employee who makes an elective deferral to your 401(k) plan. For example, the plan might provide that you will contribute 50 cents for each dollar your participating employees choose to defer under your 401(k) plan.

Eligible Rollover Distribution: Often, an eligible rollover distribution occurs when an individual leaves the service of an employer. The rollover rules allow the individual to bring the assets to their IRAs or a retirement plan at a new employer.

Read more:

http://www.investopedia.com/terms/e/eligiblerolloverdistribution. asp#ixzz2AKv6c3Xm

Enrollment Period: The time frame that someone can sign up for a qualified retirement plan.

EGTRRA (Economic Growth and Tax Relief Reconciliation Act): Law put into place in 2001 to allow for a higher rate of annual contributions for employees, and employers using profit sharing, as well as make the accounts easier to access. Among some of the changes is that this law added the "catch up" provision. Small employers are granted tax incentives to offer retirement plans to their employees, and sole proprietors, partners, and S corporation shareholders gain the right to take loans from their company pension plans.

http://www.nysscpa.org/reconciliationact/reconciliationact1.htm

Elective deferrals: The portion of an employee's salary that is contributed to a retirement plan. This could be on a pretax basis or, if the plan allows a Roth option, a post tax basis. Elective deferrals apply in the case of 401(k) plans, 403(b) annuities, SARSEPs (established before 1997), and SIMPLE plans.

ERISA: Employee Retirement Income Security Act of 1974 is a federal law that establishes minimum standards for pension plans in private industry. ERISA was enacted to protect the interests of employee benefit plan participants and their beneficiaries by requiring the financial, and other, information concerning the plan to beneficiaries. The act also established standards of conduct for plan fiduciaries. And gives the participants of these plans access to the federal courts.

Employer: An employer is any person for whom an individual performs or has performed any service, of whatever nature, as an employee. A sole proprietor is treated as his or her own employer for retirement plan purposes. In a partnership, the partnership is treated as the employer of each partner for retirement plan purposes.

Excess contribution penalty: A six-percent cumulative penalty imposed on an employer for making contributions in excess of contribution limits.

F

Fiduciary: A legal relationship of trust. A person who exercises any discretionary authority or control over the management of the plan or its assets, or who is paid to give investment advice regarding plan assets. Plan service providers such as actuaries, attorneys, accountants, brokers, and record keepers are NOT fiduciaries unless they exercise discretion or are responsible for the management of the plan or its assets.

Every plan document must clearly identify one or more persons to be the named fiduciary for the plan. If there is only one named fiduciary, that person or entity will be considered a fiduciary for all purposes under the plan. If there is more than one named fiduciary, the named fiduciaries can allocate responsibilities among themselves. The purpose of the named fiduciary designation is to clearly identify to participants and government agencies who is primarily responsible for the plan.

Fiduciaries have important responsibilities and are subject to standards of conduct because they act on behalf of participants in a retirement plan and their beneficiaries. These responsibilities include:

- ❑ Acting solely in the interest of plan participants and their beneficiaries and with the exclusive purpose of providing benefits to them;
- ❑ Carrying out their duties prudently;
- ❑ Following the plan documents (unless inconsistent with ERISA);
- ❑ Diversifying plan investments; and
- ❑ Paying only reasonable plan expenses.

Funding: In the case of defined benefit plans, the amount of assets required to be in the plan in order to meet plan liabilities (current and future pension obligations).

H

Hardship Withdrawal: Taking money out of a qualified retirement plan without penalty, when certain requirements are met. Not all plans allow hardship withdrawals; this has to be allowed by the employer. The employee can only withdrawal their own contributions, the employer contributions cannot be taken out for a hardship withdrawal. The requirements for a hardship withdrawal are as follows: It must satisfy an immediate and financial need of the employee, such as: medical expenses, the purchase of a primary residence, payment of tuition or other educational needs, payment necessary to prevent eviction.

Highly Compensated Employee: An employee who owned more than 5% of the interest in a business at any time during the year or the preceding year, regardless on compensation. This can also be defined as someone who received $115,000 in the preceding year. It is also possible to define a Highly Compensated Employee as an employee who is in the top 20% in the compensation bracket at the company.

I

In-service Distributions: This is another way to get at the money before retirement. The law will allow you to take distributions in very limited circumstances from your profit sharing plan while your business is still in operation. Those circumstances are: after participant has been on the plan for a fixed number of years (usually at least 2); after the participant reaches a certain age (which is determined by the plan); if there is an extraneous circumstance, such as a layoff, illness, disability, retirement, death or termination of employment. An in-service distribution that is moved directly into another qualified plan is considered a rollover and does not trigger a taxable event.

IRA: Retirement plan that any individual can open without the assistance of a company. Hence the term Individual Retirement Account. IRA was originally created for those that are not covered by a qualified plan. There are now 5 variations on IRA plans. All IRA plans have hefty restrictions on contribution limits and how the account can be funded.

K

Key Employee: This could be the same as a highly compensated employee in some small businesses. Someone that has a large stake in the company, an owner or partner in the company. A key employee during 2017 is generally an employee who is either of the following.

- ❑ An officer having annual pay of more than $170,000.
- ❑ An employee who is either of the following.

  - A 5% owner of your business.
  - A 1% owner of your business whose annual pay was more than $150,000.

L

Loan: A person can take out a loan from their retirement plan without penalty, if they repay it within 5 years with fixed payments and using a reasonable amount of interest. They can borrow up to $50,000 or 50% of the assets, whichever is less. , and if they qualify based on length the account has been open, person's age, and /or a hardship situation.

Leased employee: A person is considered a leased employee if they provide services to an employer according to an agreement between the employer and the leasing organization, provides services on a substantially full-time basis, and provides services under the control of the employer. For retirement plan purposes, a leased employee who is not your common-law employee must generally be treated as your employee.

M

Mandatory Minimum Distributions: Once the employee or beneficiary reaches retirement or age 70 ½, they must take out money from their account. It is required by law and mandatory, there is a "lowest amount"= Minimum, taken from an account and given to the account owner= Distribution.

If the account balance of a qualified plan participant is to be distributed (other than as an annuity), the plan administrator must figure the minimum amount required to be distributed each distribution calendar year. This minimum is figured by dividing the account balance by the applicable life expectancy. A participant must begin to receive distributions from his or her qualified retirement plan by April 1 of the first year after the later of the following years.

- ❑ Calendar year in which he or she reaches age 70 ½
- ❑ Calendar in which he or she retires from employment with the employer maintaining the plan.

However, the plan may require the participant to begin receiving distributions by April 1 of the year after the participant reaches age 70 ½ even if the participant has not retired.

Master and prototype plans: Plans typically designed by companies to be used for qualified retirement plans that comply with IRS plan requirements.

Match: What the company contributes into the retirement plan to encourage the employee to contribute. This is an amount based on what the employee contributes. There are limits to how much the employer can contribute, with the maximum being 35,000 per year per employee in 2017. The amount matched can be up to 20% of the employees wages in a sole proprietorship, partnership or LLC and 25% of the wages in a corporation.

Money Purchase Pension Plan: A simple plan that allows employers to easily plan for their expenses, because it is a set amount that they contribute. This also gives employees a sense of stability and comfort, because they know what is going to be contributed. This method does not connect the employees performance with their contribution, so may not provide the incentive that they employer would like.

N

Net earnings from self-employment: Net earnings from self-employment for SEP and qualified plans is your gross income from your trade or business (provided your personal services are a material income-producing factor) minus allowable business deductions.

For the deduction limits, earned income is net earnings for personal services actually rendered to the business. When calculating net earnings, you take into account the income tax deduction for one-half of self-employment tax and the deduction for contributions to the plan made on your behalf. The deduction for self-employment heath insurance is disregarded when figuring the deduction for one-half of self-employment tax.

Net earnings include a partner's distributive share of partnership income or loss (other than separately stated items, such as capital gains and losses). Guaranteed payments to limited partners are net earnings from self-employment as long as they are paid for services to or for the partnership. Distributions of other income or loss to limited partners and income passed through to shareholders of S Corporations are not considered net earnings from self-employment.

Nondiscrimination: Requirements to provide benefits for rank-and-file employees and not simply to favor owners and highly paid employees.

Non-elective deferral: The amount the company contributes to the Safe Harbor 401(k) plan. This is an amount that the company promises to contribute to the employee's account that is not based on a percentage of what the employee contributes.

Non-traditional investment: Investing in something outside of the normal realm of finances. This would include, but is not limited to: Real Estate, Coins (gold, silver, and platinum), Intellectual and Digital property, Art and Antiques.

Non-Qualified Retirement Plan: These are retirement funds that do not follow the guidelines and rules Congress has passed into law and thus cannot take advantage of most of the benefits a qualified plan.

Non-recourse loans: The only type of loans allowed for a retirement plan. According to rules and regulations, the holder of the account, the Self Directed IRA plan, or any business entity funded by the plan cannot be held liable for the loan repayment.

P

Participant: Any eligible employee who is covered by your retirement plan

Partner: One who shares ownership of an unincorporated trade of business with one or more persons.

Passive Income: Anything earned through an investment, such as interest or dividends earned on stocks, bonds, or savings. Something earned just buy owning something. . . no duties or actions were performed.

PBGC: The Pension Benefit Guaranty Corporation is an independent agency of the US government that was created by the ERISA to encourage the encourage the continued use of voluntary private benefit pension plans, provide timely and uninterrupted payment to pension benefits, and keep pension insurance premiums at the lowest level possible and still stay functioning. The annuity guaranteed is set. There is also an option to take out all the money in one lump sum, which is also a set amount.

Pension Protection Act: This act allows a person to make an additional 6% profit sharing contribution (up to maximum $250,000 in 2017) and may contribute $18,000 pretax into a separate 401(k) plan in 2017. This is a way to save more for retirement. The profit sharing does not count toward the 401(k) limit.

Plan Administrator: A plan administrator is responsible for determining who is eligible to participate in the plan, determining what benefits are due under the plan, and responding to benefit claims and appeals. Plan administrators also have responsibilities dictated under the Internal Revenue Code (Code) and Employment Retirement Income Security Act of 1974 (ERISA) as follows:

- ❑ Distribution of summary plan description, summary annual reports, and statement of vested benefits to participants and beneficiaries
- ❑ For plans with over 100 participants, engaging an independent qualified public accountant to audit the financial records of the plan
- ❑ Maintenance of plan records for at least six years
- ❑ Determination of whether a domestic relations order is qualified and
- ❑ Providing a written explanation of rollover and tax withholding election options, as well as an explanation of tax options with respect to distributions to recipients.

Profit Sharing Plan: A defined contribution plan where the company agrees to make substantial and recurring contributions. The contributions are flexible and usually based on the existence of profits.

Prohibited Transactions: There are some limits on what you can do with your retirement plan. Basically, it can't be used as a tool to only benefit the company. It can not be a vehicle to benefit the fiduciary or plan administrator. There is a list in Code Section 4975

Q

Qualified Domestic Relations Order (QDRO): This gives divorcing couples a vehicle to protect plan assets and minimize tax and penalties. This anti-alienation usually keeps the qualified retirement plan safe from anyone else, but in the case of divorce, the participant is able to transfer the funds to someone else (such as the soon to be former spouse).

Qualified Employee: An employee that is able to participate in a qualified retirement plan. The rules to participate must be equal for all employees, and include all employees of a particular category. If you want to provide the plan to part time employees, who work 25+ hours a week on average, then you must provide it to ALL employees who work an average of 25 hours a week or more. This program cannot be provided based on performance.

Qualified Retirement Plan: Retirement plans that offer a tax favored way to save for retirement. Qualified Retirement Plans include the QRP, 401(k)'s, Profit Sharing Plans, Money Purchases Plans, and Defined Benefit Plans. These plans were designed by the government to encourage companies to help their employees save for retirement by giving both the employee and the employer tax incentives. All Qualified Retirement Plans are regulated by ERISA and the Department of Labor, and have requirements that each plan must meet to be considered a qualified retirement plan.

A plan must offer life annuities, maintain a sufficient level of funds, administered according to the plan document, must require funds withdrawn at retirement (or age 70½, whichever comes first), the plan can not favor highly compensated employees, and must be insured by the Pension Benefit Guaranty Corporation (PBGC).

Qualified Distributions: A qualified distribution is a distribution that is made after the employee's non-exclusion period and:

- ❏ On or after the employee attains age 59 ½
- ❏ On account of the employee's being disabled, or
- ❏ On or after the employees' death

The QRP: A type of Qualified Retirement Plan that allows more flexibility than any other 401(k).

R

Rank and File Employee: The non-executive and non-managerial employees of a company.

Reporting Requirements: Any plan with assets of $250,000 or more is required to file a form 5500 with the IRS by the last day of the 7th month after the plan year ends. Any plan that has less than 100 employees and less then $250,000 in assets is exempt from filing.

Required minimum distributions: Plans must begin to distribute benefits to employees at a certain time. Generally, benefits must begin to be paid out no later that April 1 following the year in which a participant attains age 70 ½ . Failure to receive required minimum distributions results in a 50% tax on the amount not withdrawn.

Rollover: A tax free and penalty free transfer of funds and assets from one qualified plan to another on behalf of the owner.

Typically this takes place when someone leaves the employment of a company or government and had built up a 401k or another type of qualified account. There are requirements to roll money from one account to another. Usually the account owner must transfer the money from one like account to another (from traditional to traditional or Roth to Roth) to prevent any penalties or taxes being charged. Rollovers can require 20% of the account withheld if the rollover funds are distributed to the owner first and do not go directly to a new trustee.

Roth 401(k): A retirement plan that takes after tax contributions. The distributions and the fund fluctuations (interest rates, dividends, losses, etc) are all untaxed.

Roth IRA: A non-qualified retirement plan whose contributions are post tax. Original contributions can be withdrawn at any point without tax or penalty regardless of owners age. Distributions that include earnings are tax free, so long as the owner is at least 59 1/2 years old.

S

Safe Harbor: This is a type of 401(k) plan that requires everyone to be 100% vested from the beginning. This plan also requires certain minimum benefits to eligible employees either in the form of matching or non-elective contributions. This also allows for more design flexibility, and allows the employee to take out funds for loans or hardship withdrawal. *See the Honey Badger chapter*

Self- Employed Individual: Someone in business for him or herself, and whose business is not incorporated. Self-employed can include part-time work and include sole proprietors and partners.

Self-Employed Qualified Plans: The plans that people who work for themselves can open. The self-employed person can have elective deferrals and employer contributions

Slide Vesting: This is an option to vest an employee a little at a time. This means the employee has access to the money the employer (company) has put into the retirement account a certain percent each year. For Example: Say an employee starts with Company XYZ, which offers a sliding vesting of 20% a year. That means that each year the employee works for Company XYZ, they have access to 20% more of the money that Company XYZ put into the retirement account. If the employee stays at Company XYZ for 3 years, then employee can take 60% of Company XYZ's deposits (or contributions) into that account, the rest goes back to the company.

Salary reduction arrangements: Arrangements to make contributions to qualified plans from an employee's compensation on a pretax basis. In general, salary reduction arrangements relate to 401(k) plans, 403(b) annuities, SARSEPs in existence before 1997, and SIMPLE plans.

Savings incentive match plans of employees (SIMPLE): IRA- or 401(k) type plans that permit modest employee contributions via salary reduction and require modest employer contributions.

Simplified employee pensions (SEP): IRAs set up by employees to which an employer makes contributions based on a percentage of income.

Sole proprietor: A sole proprietor is an individual who owns an unincorporated business by him/herself. This includes a single member limited liability company (owned by one individual) that is treated as a disregarded entity for tax purposes. A sole proprietor is treated as both an employer and an employee for retirement plan purposes.

Stock bonus plan: Defined contribution plans that give participants shares of stock in the employer rather than cash.

Summary Annual Report (SAR): This document describes the financial information in the plan's Annual REport, the Form 5500, and is provided on an annual basis to participants in a narrative form.

Summary Plan Description (SPD): This basic descriptive document is a plain language explanation and must be comprehensive enough to apprise participants of their rights and responsibilities under the plan It also tells participants of the plan features and what to expect from the plan. For Example an SPD must include:

- ❑ When and how employees become eligible to participate;
- ❑ The source of contributions and contribution levels;
- ❑ The vesting period, i.e., the length of time an employee must belong to a plan to receive benefits from it;
- ❑ How to file a claim for those benefits; and
- ❑ A participant's basic rights and responsibilities under ERISA.

This document is given to employees after they join the plan and to beneficiaries after they first receive benefits. SPDs must also be redistributed periodically and provided on request

Summary of Material Modification (SMM): This document tells participants and beneficiaries of changes to the plan or to the information required to be in the SPD. The SMM or an updated SPD for a retirement plan must be provided to participants within 210 days after the end of the plan year in which the change was put into place.

T

Taxable Income: This is the amount that the IRS uses to determine what you will pay in income taxes. So, this is the amount before deductions, before tax deferred contributions, and the amount before taxes are taken out.

Tax-deferred: Current income that is taxed at a later date usually by putting it into a QRP or other retirement plan

Top-heavy plans: Qualified retirement plans that provide more than a certain amount of benefits or contributions to owners and/or highly paid employees. Top-heavy plans have special vesting schedules.

TPA (Third Party Administrator): This party, person or company keeps records etc.

Trustee: The person who accepts funds, manages them prudently and distributes them to the beneficiaries. A plan sponsor can either choose individual trustees - usually the owners or officers of the business - or a single institutional trustee, such as an affiliate of a bank, insurance company or other financial institution.

All plan assets must be held in a trust, and a plan trustee must be named. The trustee holds plan assets and is usually responsible for managing the plan's investments, although this function can be subject to the direction of another fiduciary, an investment manager, or plan participants. The plan trustee is usually responsible for processing contributions and investment transactions, preparing financial statements, and disbursing funds to participants or to pay fees and expenses of the trust.

U

UBIT (Unrelated Business Income Tax): the tax on unrelated business income, which comes from an activity engaged in by a tax-exempt 26 USCA 501 organization that is not related to the tax-exempt purpose of that organization. For most organizations, a business activity generates unrelated business income subject to taxation if it fails to sufficiently relate to the tax-exempt purpose of that tax exempt organization if it meets three requirements:

1. It is a trade or business,
2. It is regularly carried on, and
3. It is not substantially related to furthering the exempt purpose of the organization

§408(e)(1) states: "Any individual retirement account is exempt from taxation under this subtitle unless such account has ceased to be an individual retirement account. In addition, the IRS unequivocally confirms this in the first few paragraphs of Chapter 1 of the November 2007 revision of Publication 598 that IRAs are "subject to the tax on unrelated business income."

UDFI (Unrelated Debt-Financed Income): Income generated by an IRA or other retirement plan like the QRP through debt financing or leverage. UDFI only applies to the profit realized through debt and is based on the highest amount of leverage carried within the past 12 months.

> ❏ The QRP is EXEMPT from UDFI. An IRA is not exempt and is subject to paying the UDFI penalty tax.

An example would be if your self-directed IRA purchased a rental home in 2009 for $200,000 using a non-recourse loan with 50% down. Your IRA has secured a 80% loan to value (LTV) on the rental home. To make it easy let's assume you never paid down the principal (interest only loan). In 2017, you sold that same piece of property for $400,000. Eighty percent of the profit would be subject to UBIT because it was generated by money that was not related to the self-directed IRA. The tax is on the 80% of thes $200,000 profit, or $160,000. At current trust tax rates you're likely talking about a tax rate of 35% or more than $50,000 in tax, but not with a QRP!

Note: If the *self-directed IRA* can pay off its loan early, it may not have to pay UBIT at all. UDFI does not apply if the debt is paid off 12 months prior to the sale of the property.

If you used your QRP instead of the IRA you would not be subject to UDFI.

V

Vested: Indicates how much of the employer contributed money in the retirement plan that the employee gets to take with them, if they leave the company. There are some instances when the employee (worker) is 100% vested on day X. This would mean, the employee can take all the money that the employer (company) put into the account, once the employee has worked for that employer for X days. There is also an option to have the employee receive a percent of the money each year. For Example: For simplicities sake, let's say you make $30,000 If your employer contributes 6% of your annual income each year, they add $1800/ year. If you decide to leave that company after 3 years, you may not get the entire $5400 that the company put into the account. You have to know how much you are "vested" each year . . . what percent of that money you get to take with you. Let's say you get 20% more vested each year. When you decide to leave after 3 years, you are 60% vested. In other words, you get to keep 60% of the money that they company contributed. In this example, you would get to keep $3240 (plus whatever amount you contributed from your paycheck, that money is always yours). *See also Cliff Vesting and Slide Vesting for more information and Honey Badger Chapter for more examples.*

X

Xanadu: Where you will retire.

Y

You: The person reading this book (also see brilliant, and on your way).

Z

Zealous: How you will feel once you have opened your "The QRP" account! Ardent, enthusiastic about what a good decision this retirement plan is, eager to see your genius in play, earnest.

ARTICLES

Inherited IRAs not protected in bankruptcy

By Renee Rodda, J.D.

The Bankruptcy Court has determined that, unlike a debtor's own traditional IRA, an inherited IRA is not an exempt asset of the bankruptcy Code §522 (d) (12).

The Court concluded that funds in an inherited IRA are not funds intended for retirement purposes but, instead, are distributed to the beneficiary of the account without regard to age or retirement status.

It is generally believed that IRAs are protected in a bankruptcy proceeding, unless the funds have been used in a prohibited transaction. **The decision in this case means that taxpayers with financial difficulties may lose any inherited IRAs in a bankruptcy proceeding.**

Excluded Accounts

The bankruptcy estate includes nearly all legal and equitable rights of the debtor, as well as those interests recovered or recoverable through transfer and lien avoidance provisions. However, certain assets are specifically excluded under the Bankruptcy Code and may not be used to pay creditors.

Bankruptcy Code §522(d)(12) excluded retirement funds to the extent that those funds are in a fund or account that is exempt from taxation under IRC §§401, 403, 408, 408A, 414, 457, or 501(a).

To determine whether an account is an "exempt" retirement account, the court must determine that:

- ❏ The funds are retirement funds; and
- ❏ That the funds are exempt from tax under the specified code sections.

> **Note:** The maximum amount that can be protected in an IRA account during a bankruptcy proceeding is $1 million.

The Inherited Account

Although there is no dispute that the original IRA was a retirement account, which was exempt from taxation, the original owner's death and the distribution of the funds to her daughter transformed the nature of the IRA. Her daughter placed the distributed funds into a new IRA account created in her deceased mother's name from which she, as the beneficiary of the new account, must take distributions prior to retirement.

Even assuming that the inherited IRA contains "retirement funds," the account established by the beneficiary to receive the distribution of funds from her mother's IRA is not a traditional IRA exempt from taxation under IRC§408(e)(1). Although an inherited IRA is exempt from tax under IRC§402(c)(11), this is not one of the specific code sections listed in the bankruptcy code.

New Roth Conversion Law

On September 27, 2010, President Obama signed into law the "Small Business Jobs Act of 2010." This law contains a provision that allows 401(k) and 403(b) plans to permit participants to convert some or all of their existing pretax amounts into Roth accounts within the existing savings plan. This optional provision applies only if a savings plan allows participants to make Roth contributions. It eliminates the need for employees and spousal beneficiaries to roll non-Roth money out of their retirement plan and into a Roth IRA in order to take advantage of the Roth program.

The following types of plans are permitted to allow the Roth conversion: 401(k) Plans, 403(b) Plans, and governmental 457(b) Plans. This provision does not apply to money purchase pension plans, profit sharing plans, or defined benefit plans.

Listed below are some important facts about the Roth conversion feature:

- ❑ A Roth feature must be offered as part of the plan, in order for Roth conversions to be permitted within the plan.
- ❑ This conversation is only available to participants who have a distributable event, that would allow them to withdraw (termination, disability, death, attaining age 59½).
- ❑ This conversion applies to amounts treated as eligible rollover distributions; it disqualifies hardships, requires minimum distributions, and corrective distributions.

Section 6

FAQ'S

1. What is a Qualified Retirement Plan (QRP)?

The technical definition for a qualified plan is one that satisfies the requirements of IRC Section 401(a). A Qualified Plan is known for the numerous tax advantages the plan allows. Contributions made into the plan are not taxed until you withdraw the money, which allows an investor to save more money than in other types of retirement plans. A qualified plan is established by a business and is subject to the provisions of the Employee Retirement Income Security Act (ERISA). Some of the most common types of qualified retirement plans consist of Profit Sharing Plans, 401(k) plans, and Defined Benefit Plans

2. How many kinds of Qualified Retirement Plans are there?

There are two basic kinds of qualified plans: defined contribution plans and defined benefit plans-and different rules apply to each. You can have more than one qualified plan, but your contributions to all the plans must not total more than the overall limit.

3. Why Have a Qualified Retirement Plan?

❑ **Unlimited Options & Tax Deferral**

A QRP offers a business owner the ability to use his retirement funds to make virtually any type of investment tax-free, including real estate, on his own without requiring the consent of a custodian. The IRS only describes the disqualified investments, and very few at that! All the income and gains goes back to your QRP **tax free**!

❑ High Contribution Limits

An IRA allows you to contribute $5,500 a year, or $6,500 if you're over age 50, to "catch up." The problem with this is that you can only get $100,000 into the plan over 20 years. That's just not enough to get close to what you'll need for retirement.

With a QRP you can contribute $54,000 per person, up to $108,000 with a spouse and even more if you're over 50. ($60,000 each in 2017, if over 50 years old)

❑ Other Benefits

Qualified retirement plans can provide many tax and non-tax benefits to employers as well as to employees, such as:

- Help employers attract and retain better employees, thereby reducing turnover and new employee training costs.
- Employers can immediately deduct their contributions (within certain limits) into a qualified plan and may even be entitled to receive a tax credit for a part of the costs of implementing the plan. The balance of the cost can be deducted on your tax return.
- Employees pay no income tax on employer contributions (within certain limitations) until the funds are distributed.
- Employees benefit from the tax-free accumulation of earnings.
- Employees generally may make pretax contributions from their compensation to a qualified plan, called elective deferrals (thereby lowering participants' taxable income).
- One of the greatest advantages of qualified plans is that retirement savings from defined contribution plans are

portable. Eligible funds can be rolled over to another defined contribution plan (or IRA), in accordance with certain requirements, thereby helping employees continue to build their retirement funds and cut down on the excess paperwork caused by maintaining several retirement accounts.

- The U.S. government will even pay you back a portion of your contribution to a retirement plan up to $1,000 each year per participant for taxpayers in low tax brackets. Form 8880 is used to claim the credit.

4. How are gains handled? Can you defer through 1031? If personal/primary purchases are allowed with QRP – how are tax deductions handled?

That's the cool thing, it's automatically ALL deferred because it's inside the plan. You never buy anything that you are getting a benefit from, that's considered a disqualified investment.

5. Do I need to have a business in order to set up a plan?

No, just an intent to create income. Your business is called the plan sponsor. You have a lot of flexibility to choose the type of business you'd like to have including a sole proprietorship, LLC, Partnership or Corporation.

6. Is there a minimum amount of income my business needs before I set up my plan?

There are no minimum income limits for a QRP. You can only use your income from the business that the QRP account is associated with, but you don't have to make a certain amount.

7. What happens if I have several different businesses? Can I still use all of my income to calculate my contribution to the plan?

If you own the majority control of all your businesses, you can establish one plan and have the other businesses adopt the plan. However, if you do not have majority ownership in all the businesses, you will want to set up separate plans for each. Separate. QRP plans for each business is also beneficial if you want to be more aggressive with investments or contributions for a certain business.

8. How do I get a QRP? How long does it take?

Either visit *www.TheQRP.org* to or Call: 800-270-1649. The information required will take about 5 minutes to gather and then you'll receive your trust documents and will have your QRP within 7-10 days.

The Basic Steps in Setting UP a Qualified Retirement Plan:

- ❏ Federal ID#
- ❏ either contribute tax deductible contributions on roll over funds other
- ❏ retirement plan such as IRA, etc or elective deferrals.

9. Once my QRP is set up and I receive my plan documents how do I invest?

Set up a **bank account** at the bank or brokerage firm of your choice. You'll find an account opening sheet in your binder that you'll be able to take to the institution that will instruct them on setting up your checking or savings account. Once you have this set up you're free to invest in any allowable item by writing a check for it.

10. Do I need multiple bank accounts?

Yes, at a minimum you'll need 2 accounts one for tax referred & one for ROTH. The profit Sharing account can hold all the profit sharing for all employees. If any of the employees wishes to have part or all of their contribution classified as a ROTH contribution those monies need a separate account set up.

CONTRIBUTIONS

11. Can I Rollover my existing 401(k) or IRA into a QRP?

Yes, you can roll most IRA, SEP IRA, SIMPLE IRA (after 2 years), ROTH IRA (only into a Roth QRP, 457(b), 403(b), Profit Sharing and other QRP's into your QRP.

An IRA can be rolled into a QRP as well.

In some instances you may be able to roll funds from a 401k at a current employer through what's called an "In-Service Distribution," although most large employers are highly restrictive and make this nearly impossible.

12. Can I buy Gold and Silver with my QRP money? Can I keep the metals with me?

Yes, as long as you purchase the allowable bullion items (see the list in the Precious Metals section) you're allowed to purchase any of these you'd like. Since you're able to choose who will serve as trustee and if you choose yourself it's up to you to safeguard and hold assets as needed. In the case of precious metals you (as Trustee) are able to hold them yourself in a secure facility. The IRS requires you to be a good fiduciary of the assets, meaning you must safeguard them and protect them so it would make sense to have a secure vault or safe (which could be at your home) or a safety deposit box used to store the metals.

You must also receive regular statements of value from the broker you purchase the items from. This establishes value for reporting purposes on form 5500, the annual reporting form required by the IRS. At The Gold Bullion Guy, we provide this form to clients every quarter.

13. Can I use personal money to transfer into my plan? What money qualifies to put into the plan?

No, you cannot transfer personal money to contribute into the plan. Qualifying contributions consist of rollovers, elective deferrals, employer match contributions, employer profit sharing contributions, and qualified non-elective contributions. New deductible contributions to your plan need to be from your business account, not your personal account. They must come from wage deductions.

14. Can my significant other and I both participate in one plan?

Yes, you can both be listed as Trustees of the plan. As long as you both perform services for the company, you can make elective deferral and profit sharing contributions. In 2017, you can contribute up to $54,000 each ($108,000 if married). If you are age 50 or older, you can contribute $60,000 each.

MAINTENANCE

15. What's are the ongoing responsibilities and costs involved in a QRP Administration?

Once you're set up you'll generally have little or no ongoing expenses.

You are required to file a form 5500 with the IRS if you plan has $250,000 in assets or more. If you have less then $250,000 and less then 100 employees you're exempt from filing this form. You can file the form yourself online or you can have an advisor file the form. We recommend having an advisor file the form which costs less then $1000 a year and puts the professional in between you and the IRS, generally a smart idea.

Any asset like real estate or precious metals requires a statement of value or appraisal at least once a year to be used for compliance with plan asset value reporting. Precious metals firms generally do not do this. My Gold Advisor provides this to our clients complimentary and offers this service to anyone holding precious metals for a minimal fee.

A plan must have at least one fiduciary (a person or entity) named in the written plan, or through a process described in the plan, as having control over the plan's operation. The named fiduciary can be identified by office or by name. For some plans, it may be an administrative committee or a company's board of directors.

The duty to act prudently is one of a fiduciary's central responsibilities under ERISA. It requires expertise in a variety of areas, such as investments. Lacking that expertise, a fiduciary will want to hire someone with that professional knowledge to carry out the investment and other functions. Prudence focuses on the **process** for making fiduciary decisions. Therefore, it is wise to document decisions and the basis for those decisions. For instance, in hiring any plan service provider, a fiduciary may want to survey a number of potential providers, asking for the same information and providing the same requirements. By doing so, a fiduciary can document the process and make a meaningful comparison and selection.

16. Do I have to contribute to my QRP every year?

NO, you can contributed whenever you want with your elective deferral (your own contribution). You have a maximum that you can contribute, but no minimum requirement.

17. The actual plan doesn't have fees, but where could fees pop up?

Fees are just one of several factors fiduciaries need to consider in deciding on service providers and plan investments. When the fees for services are paid out of plan assets, fiduciaries will want to understand the fees and expenses charged and the services provided. While the law does not specify a permissible level of fees, it does require that fees charged to a plan be "reasonable." After careful evaluation during the initial selection, the plan's fees and expenses should be monitored to determine whether they continue to be reasonable.

In comparing estimates from prospective service providers, ask which services are covered for the estimated fees and which are not. Some providers offer a number of services for one fee, sometimes referred to as a "bundled" services arrangement. Others charge separately for individual services. Compare all services to be provided with the total cost for each provider. Consider whether the estimate includes services you did not specify or want. Remember, all services have costs.

Some service providers may receive additional fees from investment vehicles, such as mutual funds, that may be offered under an employer's plan. For example, mutual funds often charge fees to pay brokers and other salespersons for promoting the fund and providing other services. There also may be sales and other related charges for investments offered by a service provider. The information provided by service providers noted above should include a description of all compensation related to the services to be provided that the service providers expect to receive directly from the plan as well as the compensation they expect to receive from other sources.

Who pays the fees? Plan expenses may be paid by the employer, the plan, or both. In addition, for expenses paid by the plan, they may be allocated to participants' accounts in a variety of ways.

18. **How much more money can I save for emergencies or retirement if I take advantage of a QRP, instead of putting it into a savings account? (before taxes vs. after taxes)**

Scenario #1 and 2 show examples of investing money with a QRP by taking advantage of tax deferral opportunities inside the plan. Some IRA's also allow you to invest with pre-tax dollars. HOWEVER, they do not allow for the HUGE tax saving opportunities, investment opportunities, flexibility, hardship withdrawals, and many other key elements that are allowed in a QRP.

MORE SPECIFICS

19. **Who can be a trustee on the plan?**

You or any other person you appoint to be a trustee.

20. **Can an outside financial or legal entity (i.e. bank, law firm, CPA, trustee company, etc.) serve as trustee for a 401(k) ?**

Technically the answer is "yes," but it is not typical or financially appropriate in today's small plan marketplace, because outside trustees add additional costs to the operation of pension plans and may or may not add any benefit. Even with an outside trustee it is impossible for the employer to transfer any legal liability away from himself. The outside trustee will not reduce the employer's liabilities or responsibilities to the plan by one atom! In the past decade virtually all new small pension plans have been set-up to be self-trustee precisely because it is less expensive, and there is no benefit doing it differently.

Outside trustees typically charge 1/2 % to 1 % of the plan assets per year for their services, which amount to inspecting investment statements and certifying their accuracy. With our QRP plans, monthly statements are sent to the plan participants and employer directly from the custodian investment companies; It is both inefficient and wasteful to pay an outside trustee to certify statements that originate from an SEC-regulated custodian such as a mutual fund investment company. 401(k) Pro plans are IRS-approved to be *employer-trusteed*. (The IRS has allowed retirement plans to be employer-trusteed since 1962) .

21. Is the QRP set up with myself being the administrator, or can someone else be the administrator? What are the duties of an administrator?

You can be the administrator or hire a 3rd party to be the administrator.

Duties include:

- ❑ Make contributions in accordance to the plan.
- ❑ Keep the plan up to date and in compliance with all retirement plan laws.
- ❑ Invest plan assets in accordance to the plan.
- ❑ Provide information and required disclosures to plan participants.
- ❑ Distribute benefits in accordance with the plan.
- ❑ Inform eligible employees about the plan.

22. Under law how long must plan administer or plan provider keep 401(k)-related records?

The requirement is that records must be retained for 6 years. Records used to compile information that is required to be reported under the reporting and disclosure rules must be preserved by plan administrators (and by actuaries, accountants and others who may be involved) for 6 years after the due date for filing the documents to which they relate (ERISA Sec. 107). These records must have sufficient detail to permit the necessary basic information and data to be verified, explained or clarified for accuracy and are to include vouchers, worksheets, receipts, and applicable resolutions.

Accidental destruction of records will not discharge the persons required to retain records from their statutory duty with regard to the purposes for which such records are required to be retained. Where persons required to retain records know or should know that such reconstruction is impossible, or possible only at an excessive or unreasonable cost, such persons would not be under a duty to reconstruct or attempt to reconstruct the lost or destroyed records.

23. What investments can my QRP purchase?

- ❑ Gold Bullion coins and bars must be .9999 fine
- ❑ Silver Bullion coins and bars must be .999 fine
- ❑ U.S. Treasury Gold and Silver Coins
- ❑ Small business start ups
- ❑ Tax Lien Certificates
- ❑ Trust Deeds
- ❑ Mortgage Notes
- ❑ Single Family and Multi Unit Homes
- ❑ Securities
- ❑ CD's
- ❑ Stocks
- ❑ Bonds
- ❑ Mutual Funds
- ❑ LLC's
- ❑ Apartment Buildings
- ❑ Co-Ops
- ❑ Condominiums
- ❑ Commercial Property

- ❑ Joint Ventures
- ❑ Improved or Unimproved Land
- ❑ Commodities
- ❑ Futures
- ❑ Contracts of Sale
- ❑ Factoring
- ❑ Like and Unlike Exchanges
- ❑ Leases
- ❑ Palladium.

24. Can I buy life insurance with this plan?

Yes, you can buy life insurance with a QRP. This can dramatically cut life insurance costs by allowing premiums to be paid with mostly tax deductible rather than after tax dollars. The Tax Code also allows you to deduct the plan contributions that are used to pay for life insurance premiums. **Life Insurance is not allowed in an IRA**.

25. What investments are disallowed by the plan?

Anything considered a collectible, such as:

- ❑ Art
- ❑ Rugs
- ❑ Stamps or Collectible Coins
- ❑ Metal or Gem
- ❑ Antiques

26. Who can I invest with, are there any restrictions?

Anyone except disqualified persons. There is a list of disqualified people in question 86.

ROLLOVERS

27. What type of retirement accounts can I rollover into my new QRP?

You can roll most IRA, SEP IRA, SIMPLE IRA (after 2 years), ROTH IRA (only into a Roth QRP, 457(b), 403(b), Profit Sharing and other QRP's into your QRP.

An IRA can be rolled into a QRP if the funds in it were rolled over from a previous 401k, 403b or 457. If this is the case your IRA is considered a conduit IRA and can be rolled over into a QRP.

In some instances you may be able to roll funds from a 401k at a current employer through what's called an "In-Service Distribution," although most large employers are highly restrictive and make this nearly impossible.

28. If I have an existing 401k or IRA from an old employer, can I roll that into the new plan?

Yes. There are no taxes to pay or penalties if it is an in-kind roll over.

29. What if I retire early from my job, can I take my 401k or Profit Sharing out early and roll it over into the QRP?

Yes. This is a perfect example of where the rollover allowances are so helpful. You can roll over any retirement account into an equal account.

30. I own stocks and bonds and an IRA and want to rollover these assets to the QRP. Do I need to sell the stocks or can I roll them over to the QRP? Do you have to sell the asset first?

You do not need to sell the stocks. You can simply roll them into the QRP. This is called an In-Kind rollover.

WHAT YOU CAN DO WITH THE MONEY IN A QRP

31. Do I get complete checkbook control of the plan assets?

Yes, since you are able to serve as the administrator you select who will sign the checks for the accounts the plan holds. You would normally be the check signer. This is one of my favorite parts and probably the most significant benefit of the QRP, it doesn't require you to hire a bank or trust company to be your trustee. You, the participant can actually serve as trustee. This means that all the assets of the QRP trust are under the sole authority of the participant if you're the only participant. (If you have employees you'll still have control over your assets and the profit sharing assets with checkbook control!)

A QRP allows you to eliminate the expense and delays associated with an IRA custodian, enabling you to act quickly when the you find an investment you'd like to move on.

32. Can my QRP purchase real estate I already own?

No, you must purchase real estate initially with the plan. You can purchase new real estate with your retirement plan, but if you already own the property, there is nothing to purchase, you own it.

33. How can I invest in real estate with a QRP?

The same way you'd invest in any real estate. Once you have the QRP set up you'll have total control of your funds so anything you want to invest in you simply write a check. If you want to invest in something requiring debt you can do that as long as you're not guaranteeing it and it's non-recourse. **IRA's can't do this.**

34. Are there any restrictions on what type of property you can invest in?

There are no restrictions. You can invest in any type of property you would like, as long as you don't already own it or derive any current benefit from it.

35. Can I use debt in my investments from my plan?

Yes, qualified debt is permitted. Qualified debt is any debt that is non recourse used to purchase assets for the plan.

36. Can I personally borrow money from the plan? What are the terms of this loan?

Yes. You can borrow up to $50,000 or ½ of the vested balance, whichever is less. The loan must be amortized over a period of no more than 5 years (except for loans used to purchase a personal residence). The loan must charge a reasonable interest rate and monthly payments in substantially equal amounts must be made.

37. Can you co-mingle personal assets and bank loans with QRP funds?

NO, never co-mingle personal assets & QRP funds. This will get you into deep water with the IRS and could have your plan disqualified. If you have an investment you'd like to invest with personal funds and QRP funds you can probably do that as long as each piece is separate.

38. Can I loan family or friends money out of the plan as an investment?

You can loan money to anyone except a disqualified person (see list of disqualified parties), but the loan has to have adequate security.

You, as the trustee, must make sure the security is adequate in case of loan default.

Yes, you can make foreign investments. No, you do not have to be a U.S. citizen to have a QRP. However, you will need a US business and address

39. Does the QRP provide asset protection?

Yes, under ERISA (Employee Retirement Income Security Act) laws of 1974, the plan is protected from bankruptcy, creditors, and the IRS.

40. When do I pay taxes on my plan distributions to me personally?

The distributions are treated as income and are claimed on the tax return for that year. If the distributions are received in 2017, they are claimed to the IRS along with all other income for 2017 (e.g. April 15, 2018), and all applicable taxes will be paid at that time.

A 20% withholding is required for distributions unless the plan is a ROTH plan. A ROTH plan is not subject to withholding when a distribution is made because the distribution is 100% tax free assuming the account holder is at least 59 1/2. A rollover is not subject to taxation.

41. Do I have to file anything with the IRS when I finally start taking distributions? What is my accountant going to need for this plan?

You will need to file Form 1099R which reports income to the IRS.

Your accountant will need Form 5500 annually to report assets, contributions, and number of employees. A one person plan is exempt from filing Form 5500 is the plan assets are less than $250,000.

42. Who does the bookkeeping for my plan?

The Plan Administrator is responsible for the bookkeeping. This can be done using Quickbooks or other accounting programs for most small plans. Hiring a TPA, Third Party Administrator to serve this purpose is useful as the complexity of the plan increases. Employers often hire outside professionals (sometimes called third-party service providers) or, if applicable, use an internal administrative committee or human resources department to manage some or all of a plan's day-to-day operations. Indeed, there may be one or a number of officials with discretion over the plan. These are the plan's fiduciaries.

43. I would like to pay for the start up costs for the plan out of an existing IRA. Is this a good idea?

No, this is not a good idea because you cannot take a tax deduction if you pay for the start up costs with your IRA. If you pay using your business account, you will get a tax deduction for the cost of the plan and may even qualify for the Small Business Tax Credit.

44. How long does it take to get the plan up and running?

Once you submit your information you'll generally receive your plan documents from the firm in 7-10 days or less. Once you receive the documents, you can take them that day to open your bank account and begin making contributions.

45. How does the process work after I pay to have a plan set up?

The process is simple.

- ❑ We will prepare your plan document and mail to you once it is complete.
- ❑ You will receive two sets of signature documents. One is for you to retain for your records and the other is for our records. Sign all identified signature locations and mail back one set in the self addressed envelope provided.
- ❑ Take the complete set of plan documents, which includes your new Employer Identification Number (EIN) to any bank or financial institution and open up a bank or brokerage account for your QRP. Once the account is open, you begin making contributions from your business into your QRP or rollover funds from your IRA, 401(k), or profit sharing plan.
- ❑ You as the Trustee can begin making investments.

46. I know that congress is trying to encourage taxpayers to set up retirement plans and has passed laws to allow tax credits for startup expenses up to $500 per year for 3 years. Is this true? And how much can I write off?

Yes. The small business start up credit is 50% of eligible start up and administrative costs, for a maximum credit of $500 per year or $1500 over 3 years, plus you can write off the balance of the the cost of the plan as a business deduction. For example:

Plan cost	$2495
Year 1 tax credit:	$500
Year 1 tax deduction:	$1995
@ 40% tax bracket	<$800> savings

Out of pocket first year: $2495 - $500 - $800 = $1195

* In years 2 and 3 you can receive a tax credit up to $500 each year for administrative costs. So if you have expenses like filing a 5500 form and it cost $800, you would be able to get a tax credit of $400 from this alone.

* Savers Tax Credit: You are entitled to a tax credit of up to 50% of your contribution to a retirement plan. This provision was made a permanent part of this tax code as part of the Pension Protection Act of 2006. AGI must be less than 33,000 in 2009 for MFJ to get the full 50% *Remember*: a tax credit is a dollar for dollar reduction in your tax bill as opposed to a tax deduction. *Married couples:* get a $2,000 credit for each spouse or $4,000 total credit each year against any income taxes they owe. Saver's credit is available for IRA, QRP, 401(k), 403b, and 457 plans.

47. Is there a website I can go to for questions? Can I call you for advice on my plan and hire you later for accounting in my business?

Go to *www.TheQRP.org* for more detailed information regarding qualified retirement plans. Yes, feel free to call us for advice and hire us to handle the accounting for your business.

48. Do I have to file anything with the IRS?

YES, after your QRP is setup you will need to file Form 5500 once a year if your plan assets are over $250,000, otherwise you are exempt from mandatory filing.

49. Does the QRP have it's own Fed ID# and Separate bank account?

Yes, the Federal EIN is provided to you when the QRP is set up, the bank account is set up at the bank or brokerage of your choosing. When you receive your QRP book you'll receive a bank direction letter. If you have any troubles with a banker, you can always call us to to help.

50. What happens if I want to operate my business as a sole proprietorship now and then form an LLC or corporation later? Can I still use my old plan in the new LLC or Corp?

141

YES, that's an option. There is a 2 page adoption agreement that can be prepared for you. Your new LLC or corp can start making tax deductible contributions to the old plan just like you did before. This is complimentary at total control financial for clients.

51. **If I am not a U.S. resident (Canadian) can I set up a retirement plan in the U.S. and still keep my plan in a foreign county like Canada?**

YES. There are no laws that prevent you from having a retirement plan in both countries.

52. **When do I pay taxes on deferred income that I've contributed to my QRP?**

You'll pay taxes at your current income tax rate, which is determined by all income, including distribution income in the year that it's taken. Any portion of elective contributions identified to be ROTH (after tax contributions) will normally not have any tax owed, if distributions are done after age 59 1/2.

53. **How do I set up my new QRP bank account?**

Take federal ID # and The QRP plan documents to the bank or financial institution and open up your bank account; checking, saving, money market etc

54. **I own stocks and bonds and a IRA and want to rollover to QRP; do I need to sell the stocks or can I roll them over to the QRP?**

You do not have to sell….you simply call the current custodian of the assets and inquire into their procedure for doing a rollover into your new plan, your QRP

55. **For the 2017 year if my company is a *Sole Proprietorship, LLC or Corporation* how much time do I have to make contributions to my plan and take a tax deduction?**

You have until you file your corporate tax return in 2018, including any extensions.

56. **I have a Corporation and pay myself $30,000 annual salary. What is the maximum amount I can contribute to my plan?**

$25,000 which is a combination of elective deferral, $7,500 in profit sharing (25% x $30,000)

57. **Do you need profits in order to make contributions to a Profit-Sharing Plan?**

NO. Of course having profit would probably make it easier to actually contribute something however, contribution to a profit sharing plan is discretionary. There is no set amount of profits that you need to make to contribute to profit-sharing plans.

58. **What is a 990T?**

It's the form to report Unrelated Business Income Tax. If your QRP had active income that was taxed you would likely use this form.

59. **What are the advantages of a Qualified Plan versus an IRA?**

There are many advantages of having a Qualified Retirement Plan versus and IRA. Please refer to exhibit 2 titled "Advantages of a Qualified Plan vs an IRA".

60. What types of businesses can set up Qualified Retirement Plans?

Sole Proprietorship, C Corporation, S Corporation, Partnership, Limited Liability Corporation (LLC), Limited Liability Partnership (LLP), and Not for Profit 501(c)(3).

SELF DIRECTED 401(K)/ The QRP

61. What is a self-directed 401(k) such as The QRP?

A self-directed 401(k) is technically no different than any other 401(k). It's unique because of the available investment options. Most custodians only allow approved stocks, bonds, mutual funds and CDs. A truly self-directed 401(k) allows those types of investments PLUS specific gold and silver, real estate, notes, private placements, tax lien certificates and much more.

62. What are the benefits of The QRP?

In addition to the tremendous 401(k) benefits already discussed (tax-free profits, tax deductions, asset protection and estate planning), you can invest tax-free in investments that you know and understand, which through the power of compounding interest, can create additional wealth for you and your family.

63. Are there any negatives of The QRP?

The QRP does require more administration than something like an IRA. Since you, the business owner, will typically be the trustee in a QRP, you have a fiduciary responsibility to protect assets. This responsibility is not normally required in an IRA that has a third party custodian.

64. Why haven't I heard of The QRP before?

While the concept of investing in real estate and other assets in retirement plans has been around for more than 30 years, it hasn't received a great deal of attention. Why? Most custodians that offer 401(k)s (banks and brokerage firms) focus on mutual funds and CDs-because they have financial interests in having you select those investments from them. Meaning, they make money by directing and managing the investments for you. The idea here is to be in control of your own financial success.

Because a majority of custodians focus on stocks and CDs, there's a common misconception that these are your only investment options for retirement plans. But this is not the case.

65. Is The QRPs allowed under IRS rules?

Yes, as long as you follow relevant rules. IRS Publication 560 and 590 clearly state the rules and regulations governing IRAs and qualified retirement plans. You can find these publications on *www.TheQRP.org/560* and *www.TheQRP.org/590* respectively.

66. Are there special rules for The QRP investments?

Yes. To ensure compliance, you should be familiar with specific rules for 401(k)'s and in particular, self-directed 401(k)s. There are certain types of transactions that you cannot perform through a 401(k). Most importantly, the IRS prohibits "self-dealing" investments in which you or family members of lineal descent have prior ownership.

67. How can I be sure that my investment is allowable in a QRP?

IRS Publications state what investments are prohibited in Qualified Retirement Plans. These investments include: artwork, stamps, rugs, antiques and gems.

All other investments, including stocks, bonds, mutual funds, real estate, promissory notes, foreclosures, and tax liens are acceptable as long as IRS rules governing retirement plans are followed.

68. My CPA/attorney/financial advisor hasn't heard of The QRP? What Should I Do?

It's not uncommon for advisors to never have heard of self-directed qualified retirement plans. We have worked with many professional advisors across the country to educate them regarding QRP's and self directed QRP rules so they can give good financial advice to their clients.

69. Are my self directed QRP investments guaranteed?

No investment (aside for FDIC-insured deposits) is guaranteed. However, most successful investors feel that the risk of investing in assets they know and understand is much less than the risk associated with making only conventional investments.

70. Are self directed QRP's for everyone?

Self directed QRPs are not for everyone. They are generally better for those who want to create wealth by using their knowledge of investing in assets other than stocks, bonds and CDs.

71. What are the Prohibited transactions?

Prohibited transactions are listed in Code Section 4975 are transactions between the plan and a disqualified person that are prohibited by law. *However see Exemption later.* If you are a disqualified person who takes part in a prohibited transaction, you must pay a tax. Prohibited transactions generally include the following transactions:

- ❑ A transfer of plan income or assets to, or use of them by or for the benefit of, a disqualified person.
- ❑ Any act of a fiduciary by which he or she deals with plan income or assets in his or her own interest.
- ❑ The receipt of consideration by a fiduciary for his or her own account from any party dealing with the plan in a transaction that involves plan income or assets.
- ❑ Examples of some common Prohibited Transactions:
- ❑ Selling an interest in real estate owned by the QRP to a "Disqualified Person"
- ❑ Buying an interest in real estate for your QRP from a "Disqualified Person"
- ❑ Selling or transferring real estate you own personally to your QRP
- ❑ Purchasing real estate with QRP funds and leasing to a disqualified person
- ❑ Investing QRP funds in a house that is used by the QRP owner or other "Disqualified Person"
- ❑ Personally guaranteeing a loan to your QRP
- ❑ Buying real estate with your QRP and making repairs personally or having a "Disqualified Person" make them
- ❑ Buying real estate with personal funds and then transferring title to the QRP
- ❑ Using personal funds to pay taxes and expenses related to the QRP plan real estate investment
- ❑ Being compensated for any services performed for or on behalf of the QRP
- ❑ Contributing personal funds to your QRP bank account
- ❑ Acquiring a credit card for your QRP bank account
- ❑ Using your retirement funds to make a real estate investment and earning a commission personally from the purchase.
- ❑ Making an investments using your QRP into a company or fund that will benefit the QRP participant or a "Disqualified Person" personally
- ❑ Making an investment using QRP funds to facilitate or protect the QRP owners's investment

Any of the following acts between the plan and a disqualified person

- Selling, exchanging, or leasing property between a plan and a disqualified person
- Lending money or extending credit between a plan and a disqualified person
- Furnishing goods, services, or facilities between a plan and a disqualified person
- Transfer to or use by or for the benefit of a disqualified person of the income or assets of a plan
- Act by a disqualified person who is a fiduciary whereby he deals with the income or assets of a plan in his own interests or for his own account; or
- Receipt of any consideration for his own personal account by any disqualified person who is a fiduciary from any party dealing with a plan in connection with a transaction involving the income or assets of the plan.

EXEMPTION: Certain transactions are exempt from being treated as prohibited transactions. For example: a prohibited transaction does not take place if you are a disqualified person and receive any benefit to which you are entitled as a plan participant or beneficiary.

72. Who is a Disqualified Persons?

A Disqualified Person according to Internal Revenue Code Section 4975(e)(2) generally includes the QRP participant, any ancestors or lineal descendants (kids or their offspring) of the plan participant, and entities in which the plan participant holds a controlling equity or management interest. Under this section a "disqualified person" means:

- A fiduciary (the QRP plan participant, or person having authority over making plan investments.

- ❑ A person providing services to the plan (ex. the trustee or custodian)
- ❑ An employer, any of whole employees are covered by the QRP
- ❑ An employee organization any of whose members are covered by the QRP
- ❑ A 50 percent owner of C or D
- ❑ A family member of A, B, C or D above the lineal descendants (the participant or fiduciary's spouse, parents, grandparents, children, grandchildren, spouses of the fiduciary's children and grandchildren, but not parents in law or siblings)
- ❑ An entity (corporation, partnership, trust or estate) owned or controlled more then 50% by A, B, C, D, or E. Whether an entity is a disqualified person is determined by considering the indirect stockholdings/interest which would be taken into account under Code Sec. 267(c), except that members of a fiduciary's family are the family members under Code Sec. 4975(3)(6) (lineal descendants) for purpose of determining disqualified persons.

* Siblings, aunts, uncles, cousins, step siblings or friends are not treated as "Disqualified Persons"

For More information on Retirement Plans for Small Businesses please see:

http://www.irs.gov/pub/irs-pdf/p560.pdf

http://www.irs.gov/Retirement-Plans/Plan-Participant,-Employee/401(k)-Resource-Guide---Plan-Participants---Limitation-on-Elective-Deferrals

Thank you for investing the time reading this book.

For additional information on the QRP,
inquires about bulk purchases or to contact
the author for any other reason please visit:

www.TheQRPBook.com
or
call 800-270-1649

You'll also be able to set a QRP up here.

Thank you for reading this.

—Damion Lupo